SPELLBUND

SPELLBOUND

The Seven Magic Techniques of
Influence, Persuasion and Success

DAVID KWONG
Illusionist, puzzle master and TED speaker

1 3 5 7 9 10 8 6 4 2

Virgin Books, an imprint of Ebury Publishing,
20 Vauxhall Bridge Road,
London SW1V 2SA

Virgin Books is part of the Penguin Random House group of companies whose addresses
can be found at global.penguinrandomhouse.com

Copyright © David Kwong 2017

David Kwong has asserted his right to be identified as the author of this Work in
accordance with the Copyright, Designs and Patents Act 1988

First published in the United Kingdom by Virgin Books in 2017
First published in the United States by HarperCollins in 2017

www.penguin.co.uk

A CIP catalogue record for this book is available from the British Library

ISBN 9780753557358

Printed and bound in Great Britain by Clays Ltd, St Ives PLC

Penguin Random House is committed to a sustainable future for our
business, our readers and our planet. This book is made from
Forest Stewardship Council® certified paper.

TO MY PARENTS AND MY BROTHER—
JOANIE, TAI, AND MICHAEL,

THANK YOU FOR YOUR LOVE, SUPPORT,
AND THE LITERALLY *THOUSANDS* OF
CARDS THAT YOU'VE PICKED.

CONTENTS

INTRODUCTION: THE BUSINESS
OF ILLUSION

Many magicians pretend to have superpowers. They strive to convince spectators that their feats are impossible for mere mortals to comprehend, let alone imitate. Often they claim to have extrasensory or telepathic abilities. Not all illusionists play these games, however. There are those—far fewer in number—who freely acknowledge that their powers are the product of tricks and of years of study. I fall into this latter camp.

Though I, too, pride myself on giving my audiences the thrill of disbelief, of mystery and a sense of the impossible, I don't pretend that the power of illusion is supernatural. On the contrary, I understand and insist that *magic actually takes place in the mind of the spectator*. It's a deeply and fundamentally human process, which is why those who command the true power of illusion are masters, not of ESP, but of insight and influence.

I practice illusionism as entertainment. My audiences range from corporate CEOs to TED talk viewers, and my stock in trade consists of cards and crossword puzzles, ordinary objects and information encoded in the minds of volunteers. I don't pull rabbits from hats, or use smoke and mirrors. I don't vanish tigers, or levitate scantily clad women. My foremost advantage as a magician is that I'm always one step ahead (or two or three or four). My hand is quicker than your eye. I know what you'll notice, and what you won't. I employ *science* to conjure feats that only appear impossible.

The original sorcerers used the very same tricks, though most would have rather been burned at the stake than admit it. Magic's roots stretch back to the occult and shamanistic rituals of high priests, astrologists, and oracles, many of whom used supposedly psychic gifts to direct the conduct of emperors and kings. The ability to hold a royal audience spellbound often led to political power. The sorcerers' currency was awe, and their audiences were willing to pay dearly for it.

As the saying goes, the more things change, the more they stay the same. Our lives today may appear to be dominated more by global technology than by royal sorcerers, but illusion still plays a fundamental role in *all* human thought. Every one of us relies on illusory information to help us decide what is true and what's false, who is trustworthy and who's not, what the future will hold, and what our options are. Arguably, the principles of illusion have never played a stronger role in determining our leaders, policies, and success stories than they do today.

When Steve Jobs introduced the Apple II, didn't he have to create an illusion of novelty that telegraphed the exceptionalism of his improvements on Apple I? When Maestro Gustavo Dudamel raises his baton to conduct the Los Angeles Philharmonic, doesn't he project an illusion of absolute readiness that will override any hesitation among his orchestra members? And when Warren Buffett is bucking trends that dominate Wall Street, mustn't he simultaneously deploy an illusion of certainty to compel his investors to trust his wisdom and leadership? Business and thought leaders as diverse as Ted Turner and President Obama, Megyn Kelly and Jeff

Bezos, have used the principles of illusion to sway opinions and secure power and influence. Some CEOs, such as Kind Snacks' Daniel Lubetzky, Aaron Levie of Box.net, Supplemental Health Care's Janet Elkin, and Tony Hsieh of Zappos, literally performed as magicians before entering the corporate world. But whether or not they've ever conducted stage illusions, all successful executives are masters of control and agents of command. They understand how the human brain is wired to fill the gap between seeing and believing—and they take advantage of that wiring for their own purposes.

Ultimately, compelling leaders know how dependent their audiences are on illusion, and they use that knowledge to impress, persuade, and motivate. Just as you can.

There is no official instruction manual for practicing illusion. However, in this book I've distilled the methods I use onstage into seven core principles that have centuries of beta-tested success behind them. These seven fundamentals empower magicians to command a room, to build anticipation, and to *appear* to work wonders. They keep us at least one step ahead of the audience, showcasing our abilities and converting skeptics into supporters. But you don't have to be a magician to master these principles. And you needn't be an entertainer to benefit from them. On the contrary, they can be game changers for you in any arena—political, corporate, technological, even in your social life.

In the chapters that follow you'll learn the rules of human behavior and cognition that make your audience susceptible to illusion. You'll meet thought leaders and innovators throughout history who have used these tenets to leverage their ideas into industry empires. And you'll discover how these seven principles can give you an edge on the competition and grant you a greater sense of control in your own life.

You know how cutthroat the world is today. Everyone is trying to land a better job, obtain the green light for their project, attract more customers, clients, and friends. Everyone wants to get ahead—and everyone is trying in the same way. That's their problem. But the principles of illusion will give you a different approach to sell your idea, product, or skills, making your best shot better than everyone else's.

Let me be clear: I'm not going to teach you how to perform specific magic tricks. For ages, the best of these acts have been handed down from masters to apprentices, from fathers to sons through generations of family trade. This practice is considered so sacred that, for lack of a suitable heir, the pioneering Austrian magician Johann Nepomuk Hofzinser actually ordered his own priceless library destroyed upon his death in 1875. The reason for this secrecy is simple: Knowing exactly how a trick works undermines the illusion. It wrecks the trade. And it ruins the mystery. I would never explain anyone else's trade secrets. I'm not going to rob you of the joy of watching a magic show. And I'm not going to teach you how to become a magician—though I do believe you'll appreciate the art of illusion more when you understand its underlying principles.

Nor am I going to show you how to cheat. It is in the nature of magic to deceive, and the line between illusion and con artistry can be slippery, but the purpose of this book is most definitely *not* to serve as a guide for conning people. On the contrary, I want to emphasize that the more you make your audience believe, the greater your responsibility becomes for the effects of that belief.

Illusion is a powerful business. Between your designs and the other person's awe, there will always be a certain amount of manipulation. If your manipulations are intended to enrich or empower yourself at your audience's expense, that could qualify as a con. On the other hand, if you use illusion as a tool to legitimately educate or assist your audiences, then you'll deserve to be regarded as a hero. Consequences count.

Magic asks you to question what you see before you and envision what can't possibly be there. To harness the power of the magical gap between what is and what could be, for your own *ethical* purposes—that is the real business of this book. As a bonus, you'll learn how to spot a con and protect yourself from the dirty tricks of fraudsters! The best defense is an educated offense, especially when dealing with illusions.

W hat I *will* reveal to you are the seven essential principles that form the foundation for illusion in magic and in life. In the chapters to come you'll learn how and why to approach your goals as a magician would:

1. In *Mind the Gap*, you'll learn to recognize and employ the perceptual space between your audience's ability to see and their impulse to believe.

2. In *Load Up*, I'll help you prepare to amaze your audience.

3. In *Write the Script*, you'll discover the importance of shaping the narrative that surrounds your illusion.

4. In *Control the Frame*, we'll explore the real-life value of a magician's best friend: misdirection.

5. In *Design Free Choice*, you'll learn the illusionist's technique of commanding your audience by giving *them* agency.

6. In *Employ the Familiar*, I'll show you how to take secret advantage of habits, patterns, and audience expectations.

7. Finally, in *Conjure an Out*, you'll learn how to develop backup plans that will keep you one, two, three, or more steps ahead of the competition.

In the pages to come you'll also meet a host of business, political, and thought leaders, from FBI negotiators to social networking mavens, from tech entrepreneurs to corporate CEOs, who've applied these principles to solve problems, inspire followers, and win the support they most need to succeed. I'll introduce you to figures throughout history, not just legendary magicians, but also heads of state and ancient power brokers who used these same principles to win wars, subdue enemies, and build nations. Most important of all, you'll learn how to apply these principles to the challenges you face in your own career and personal life.

To benefit from the art of illusion you don't need to learn how to palm cards or saw a trusting volunteer in half. All you need are these seven principles. No top hat necessary!

SPELLBOUND

MIND THE GAP

Michael Scot was a man who navigated the gap between science and illusion with extraordinary fluency. Born circa 1175, the Scottish mathematician, philosopher, and astronomer became famous in his day for divining the future based on planetary position and motion. Then he traveled to foreign lands, where he translated Muslim and Hebrew texts into Latin. People back in Britain began to associate him with the mysticism that he interpreted.

It was said that Scot tamed a devil by giving him the neverending task of making rope out of the sand of Kirkcaldy beach; that he captured the plague and locked it deep within a vault in Glenluce Abbey. He supposedly summoned a demon-horse, which he commanded to stomp its hoof three times: The first stomp made the bells of Notre Dame ring; the second caused the palace towers to crumble to the earth; and before the third blow, the French king acquiesced to Scot's demands that the French plundering of Scottish ships cease.[1] Michael Scot had some serious power, and not all of it was fictional.

In 1223, Pope Honorius III offered Scot the position of archbishop of Cashel, and four years later Pope Gregory IX tried to make him archbishop of Canterbury. Although Scot declined both appointments, he continued to travel in illustrious circles. Frederick II, the Holy Roman Emperor and king of Sicily, warmly welcomed the philosopher-magician into his court as imperial tutor to teach him the scientific laws of the universe—including augury.[2] Scot was not the first, and he wouldn't be the last to turn the art of illusion into an instrument of power, but he was one of the few real-life Merlins to hold so many reigning kings and popes spellbound.

My own introduction to the hidden benefits of illusion might seem laughably modest next to Michael Scot's, but mine involved a hero who was no less than a king in my eyes: the incomparable Will Shortz.

It was January 1, 2010. I was thirty years old and meeting the *New York Times* puzzle master for the second time in my life. We'd first met when I was a teenager, after Shortz gave a talk at the Wellfleet public library on Cape Cod. Already then a card-carrying member of the National Scrabble Association, I successfully converted LACKIES + P to SPECIAL K during the audience participation segment, and Shortz made my year by inscribing a dedication in my book of *Games* magazine puzzles: "To David, a puzzle 'champ.'" It wasn't long before I began corresponding with the guru of games through my own crossword submissions to the *Times*, and eventually this magnanimous wordsmith even accepted a few. But we hadn't met in person again, until this New Year's Day.

SPELLBOUND

We were to play table tennis. Shortz had once been told by a neurobiologist that table tennis activates all parts of the brain that crosswords do not, though, like puzzle construction, the game requires both a driven pursuit of excellence and a desire to command the person on the other side of the net. So for more than three decades Shortz had been an avid player and tournament competitor. He believed that if "every day I do puzzles and table tennis, I'm getting an all-around brain workout." In 2009, he'd founded the Westchester Table Tennis Center, the largest of its kind in North America and the site of our first match.

But I had a hidden agenda. I had a trick—literally—up my sleeve, as well as in my pockets, where I'd concealed a deck of cards, a kiwi fruit, a knife, a Sharpie, and some invisible string. Jeans and a button-down long-sleeved shirt were required to hide this cache, but they made the worst possible outfit for professional-level table tennis. Shortz, whose athletic prowess was the result of thousands of hours of drilling, repetition, and trial and error, predictably wiped the floor with me. In three games I won just two points. But then came my chance to redeem myself.

I asked Will if he'd like to see some magic, and he enthusiastically summoned a crowd to the reception area, where I served up one of my standard "openers." First, I made four jacks appear from my bare hands. Then, with a twist of the palm, they turned to aces. After this quick and flashy start, I handed over the kiwi fruit for audience inspection. Separately, I asked Shortz to sign a dollar bill, which a wave of my hand turned into one thousand Korean won. Though he probably lost about fourteen cents on that transaction, he was nevertheless pleased by the transformation. Next, I returned to the deck and asked several spectators to choose a playing card for what is known as a "multiple selection routine." Ten cards were taken, and through a variety of dexterous cuts, flashy waterfall shuffles, and pop-out moves, I located each and every card. For the finale, I asked Shortz to slice open the kiwi, and inside he found his one-dollar bill, covered in seeds and juice but still bearing his signature.

The puzzle master was gobsmacked! My hero, the encyclopedic guru of all things enigmatic and puzzling, couldn't figure out a single one of my illusions.

This was the moment when the ultimate value of magic crystallized for me. My skill was like a secret key. Magic made me impressive and memorable, just as it had Michael Scot. It garnered interest and respect, even from the most exalted of audiences. What I'd glimpsed was the inherent power of illusion as a force for personal command.

To be sure, magic typically distills this power into an art form that impresses in order to entertain audiences, but the more I thought about it, the more I realized that illusion exerts its influence over virtually every field of human activity, from politics and religion to science and industry. So success in *any* field requires mastery of the principles of illusion.

THE PERCEPTUAL GAP

Instinctively, we humans believe what we observe with our own eyes. We trust our senses and our powers of perception. We assume that we're smart and alert enough to distinguish the real deal from the phony, and we have faith in our ability to tell a smart idea from a stupid one, an upright citizen from a cheat, a genius from a wannabe. *Seeing is believing.* This equation guides our choice of friends and mates, of our most trusted employees, advisors, and leaders. It helps us decide where to live, how to vote, and what to buy. It's in our DNA.

If we weren't wired this way, we couldn't function. We'd have no ego, no self-confidence, no courage. If we didn't trust our senses to guide us, we'd probably never get out of bed. But while our faith in our own perceptiveness allows us to act decisively and take calculated risks, it also leaves us vulnerable to illusion. That's because our perceptions are riddled with blind spots—gaps that our mind fills automatically with assumptions that can be logical, or magical, or as misleading as a mirage of water shimmering over a desert highway.

Consider the simple flip, or "flick" book, which was a precursor to animation and film. A series of pages are drawn to show a progression of images, like Mickey Mouse in "Steamboat Willie." Then the drawings are bound so the pages can be flipped to create the *illusion* of a single, seamlessly moving picture. The illusion works because our brains fill the gaps between the pages, allowing our minds to "see" more than our eyes can.

The same wiring allows us as kids to "see" the suggested picture even before drawing the lines in connect-the-dots puzzles. It allows us to admire images of water lilies, haystacks, and families picnicking on the grass in paintings by Impressionist painters that actually consist of tiny disconnected spots of paint. It also allows us to read by bridging the gaps between letters to form words, between words to form sentences, between sentences to "see" larger ideas, arguments, and stories. Without your brain's natural aptitude for illusion, this page would simply appear to you as a bunch of black squiggles on a white background.

Illusionists take full advantage of the processes by which the mind connects the dots of perception. One of these is called *amodal completion*. You see the front of a dachshund to one side of a tree trunk, and the hind end to the other side, and you mentally picture the whole continuous dog behind the tree. That's amodal completion at work. A magician, however, would know that it's also possible to position *two* dogs (perhaps even more) behind the tree, or maybe two stuffed *half* dogs. This same magician could then blow your mind by "stretching" the dachshund to a seemingly impossible length, or by "cutting the dog in half," all by exploiting the gap between what you truly can see and what you assume.

KANIZSA'S TRIANGLE

Illusory contours are visual illusions in which your brain fills the gap with edges because of clues instead of changes in light. One of the more famous examples of an illusory contour is Kanizsa's Triangle, created by Italian psychologist Gaetano Kanizsa in 1955:

The upside-down triangle does not exist, but your mind perceives a solid shape even though there are no enclosed spaces. The Kanizsa Triangle is emblematic of Gestalt psychology, which centrally holds that "the whole is greater than the sum of its parts." In other words, in this chaotic world where we are bombarded by visual stimuli, our mind organizes perceptions into meaning. Thus, where there are incomplete objects, we see them as whole. Where there are gaps, we fill them with contours to create shapes we can recognize.

But the role of illusion in our lives extends way beyond vision. When we listen to an orchestra we hear a single unified piece of music, rather than sixty separate instruments. Even when we read a mangled line such as, *Fr scre and svn yrs ago or fthrs brt frth on ths cntnnt, a nw ntion, cncved in Lbrty, nd dedcted to th prpsition tht ll mn ar creted equl,* we have little difficulty filling in the missing vowels and recognizing the beginning of the Gettysburg Address. When we take a bite of yellow cake we register the overall taste of cake, rather than the separate flavors of salt, flour, eggs, butter, milk, vanilla, and sugar. The larger general impression quickly overwhelms any notice of the individual component ingredients— unless you happen to be a connoisseur like some culinary taste testers who have trained themselves to notice the micro flavors within the macro.

Our cognitive tendency to fill in gaps also dominates our ability to solve problems and read character, using what we *do* know to help us make assumptions about what we *don't*—assumptions that we then view as reliable facts. This can easily lead to unintended consequences, as some British voters discovered in 2016 after casting a "protest vote" for the United Kingdom to leave the European Union. Prior to the referendum, national polls showed that the majority of voters preferred to remain in the EU, which led many disgruntled citizens to assume that their "leave" vote wouldn't matter. They merely wanted to voice their frustration against the British government. The day after the Leave campaign won, many had voters' remorse. One BBC reporter tweeted, "most told us they woke up thinking 'what have I done?' & didn't actually expect the UK to leave."[3]

In business, entrepreneurs who are mindful of the gap between their own practices and assumptions can avoid such unwelcome surprises. They also tend to think more creatively and proactively. Aaron Levie, who was a kid magician before he founded the online file storage company Box.net, suggests, "Look at the organization and figure out what's missing. Ask, where are *our* gaps? Where are our weaknesses? And then, how do we solve for those things?" The mistake many companies make, he says, is to concentrate exclusively on their strengths. While it's important to identify your strengths, to develop and invest in those areas, "it's really important that you constantly know why you *wouldn't* succeed, and what you need to do to change that." Don't get trapped, in other words, by the illusion that you're bulletproof.[4]

What we "know" about other people can be even more misleading. Just ask anyone who's ever been fooled in love, or surprised by a friend's "uncharacteristic" behavior, or taken in by a charismatic pitch person. Whether or not we realize it, illusion plays a role in virtually every human interaction, as well as in every decision we make and everything we do.

SPELLBOUND

Instead of being blindsided by the gap between assumptions and facts, illusionists of all stripes, from magicians to savvy politicians to visionary entrepreneurs, take advantage of this fundamental human reality. They use it to impress, persuade, motivate, and lead their audiences, to shape what other people think they see, and to direct what they feel and believe.

British illusionist Derren Brown is totally up front about this. "Much, if not all, of conjuring relies on the performer creating a false trail of events that clearly leads to a particular climax," he explains. "The magician creates a very strong sense of A leads to B leads to C leads to D, where A is the start of the trick and D is the impossible climax."[5] But that causal connection is not necessarily real. Although it's been engineered by the magician, "it exists only in the head of the spectator." Which is to say that magic takes place *between* what's known and what's believed.

Daniel Lubetzky, CEO of Kind Snacks, is another entrepreneur whose leadership practices are influenced by his history as a teen illusionist. "The thing I love the most about magic," he says, "is that you're creating something new, something surprising, something different. . . . You learn so much about fundamental human relations and how to relate to one another, and how to get them to pay attention to what you want. . . . We try to create magical solutions and think outside the box in everything we do at Kind. It really follows from, as a kid, learning how to surprise and delight people with something that they were not expecting."[6]

This is the power that so thrilled me when I stymied Will Shortz.

But long before that, I knew that illusion had power over *me*. As a kid I devoured beginners' books on the subject—*The Klutz Book of Magic*, Bill Tarr's *Now You See It, Now You Don't!*, and eventually the bible of card sleights, *The Royal Road to Card Magic*. I practiced illusions obsessively throughout my teens, and then, as a wide-eyed freshman at Harvard, I attended a lecture given by the great historian of magic Ricky Jay.

That afternoon the university's ivy-covered Agassiz Theatre was packed, buzzing with excitement from the legendary sleight-of-hand master's fans. Jay was speaking about nineteenth- and early-twentieth-century lithographs in conjunction with "The Imagery of Illusion: Nineteenth Century Magic and Deception," an exhibit he'd curated at the Harvard Theatre Collection at Pusey Library. He told tales of Herrmann the Great, Carter the Great, and Chung Ling Soo—illusionists who were widely believed to have supernatural abilities.

I was so inspired by Jay's stories that the very next week I marched into Robinson Hall and declared the history of magicians and vaudeville as my concentration (Harvard's pompous term for a major). Over the ensuing semesters I learned that the special relationship between illusion and the power to direct emotions and beliefs extends far beyond flip books.

THE ILLUSIONIST AS DIRECTOR

The best example of the directorial power of illusion is the motion picture industry, which in many ways grew out of stage magic. One of the earliest filmmakers, Georges Méliès (portrayed in Martin Scorsese's 2011 film, *Hugo*), was an illusionist who'd bought the

Théâtre Robert-Houdin from the famous magician Jean Eugène Robert-Houdin, whose name Harry Houdini would later borrow. On December 28, 1895, Méliès attended a special demonstration of the Lumière brothers' cinematograph—an early motion picture camera that also functioned as a projector—and he was smitten.

Méliès recognized the same potential that the legendary director Ingmar Bergman would describe a century later when writing about the "little rickety machine" projector that he called his "first conjuring set" because it allowed him to take advantage of "the blankness between the frames" to sway his audience's emotions— "make them laugh, scream with fright, smile, believe in fairy stories."[7] To direct audience emotions, in other words, by minding the gaps of cognition.

Seeing this same promise in his own little rickety machine, Méliès soon had the Théâtre Robert-Houdin projecting Thomas Edison's one-minute shorts before packed houses. But Méliès was not content with those first films' straightforward footage of athletes and parades. Like Bergman, he wanted to orchestrate the frames of film to move people emotionally. And as an innovator, he saw that, while certain principles of illusion were built into this new technology, still others could be transferred from stage magic to create novel special effects. As a visionary, he recognized that the power of illusion is unlimited.

Méliès honored his love of magic by using theatrical acts of illusion as the subject for many of his early films. They also inspired many of the cinematic effects he masterminded. In 1896, for instance, he directed and starred in *Escamotage d'une dame chez Robert-Houdin*, or *The Vanishing Lady*, which reinvented a spectacle that the magician Buatier de Kolta had made famous at London's Egyptian Hall. On celluloid Méliès enhanced the story by using a "stop trick"—turning off the camera while a change is made—to seemingly transform the woman on-screen into a skeleton before making her reappear. This special effect, possible only in the new medium of film, allowed him to turn a simple illusion into an existential story of life and mortality. Over the course of making more than five hundred films, he would go on to experiment with multiple exposures, time-lapse photography, dissolves, and painted film—all variants of magic that touched the human heart.

Georges Méliès understood that movies and illusion both involve "controlled perspective." When directors hold their fingers in two L shapes to create a frame, they are in effect re-creating the proscenium of the magician's stage. And by adjusting the audience's perception of the world within that frame, they can deliver surprise and amazement, which in turn establishes them as forces of ingenuity, talent, and influence. In this sense, all directors are illusionists, and all illusionists, whether they be magicians, CEOs, salespeople, or bloggers, are directors.

ILLUSION IN THE ART OF BUSINESS

It's no wonder, given this connection between illusion and cinema, that I was drawn to Hollywood. After graduating from college, I made a beeline for the entertainment industry and began juggling magic gigs and entry positions at companies like HBO and Dream-Works Animation. I discovered with glee that one of the greatest directors of all time, Orson Welles, had also been an accomplished magician. "Orson the Magnificent" sawed Marlene Dietrich in half as part of his *Mercury Wonder Show for Service Men* during World War II. He demonstrated his magic tricks on-screen in *Follow the*

Boys (1944), *Magic Trick* (1953), and *Casino Royale* (1967), and was working on *Orson Welles' Magic Show* for television when he died in 1985.

More recently, another kid magician, J. J. Abrams, grew up to be the prolific director of blockbusters such as *Star Trek, Super 8, Mission: Impossible III,* and *Star Wars: The Force Awakens.* The linkage was no more coincidental for Abrams than it was for Welles. An original sign from Tannen's Magic, a legendary Manhattan magic shop, is prominently displayed at Bad Robot, Abrams's production company, and he keeps in his office a "mystery box" from Tannen's ("mystery" as in grab bag; the contents were not revealed on the package) that he's had for more than thirty years and never opened. Magic and mystery, Abrams has said, represent "infinite possibility."[8]

Thinking "outside the box," then, means protecting and working around the mystery of what's inside. In terms of illusion, it means protecting and *employing* that gap between what we can see and what we can't, between what we perceive and what we believe.

I n 2009, I learned about a screenplay that was being developed about a vigilante gang of magicians who operate like superheroes. I jumped at the opportunity to get involved and became *Now You See Me*'s lead magic consultant, collaborating with the screenwriters to devise original methods for how the heroes could use illusion to pull off bank heists. When Lionsgate gave the production the green light, I moved to New Orleans to create illusions on set and teach the actors sleight of hand.

What the filmmakers really wanted to highlight was how a magician thinks. We wove tenets like misdirection and being "ahead" into the plot to give audiences a peek behind the curtain of illusion. That way they could better understand the actions of the magician heroes—and root for them.

Even then, though, I had more to learn about the magic of cinema. One steamy Louisiana evening we were shooting an opening scene in which Jesse Eisenberg is charming a young woman with his sleight of hand. He was supposed to move his hand along a neon tube, transforming the gas-filled glass into a sparkling necklace, but the execution was too difficult, and I was out of tricks. Noticing my panic, director Louis Leterrier pulled me aside and told me, "Don't worry. I'm a magician too." In other words, he could control where people looked and what they remembered by adjusting the pace of a scene or moving the camera quickly through a sequence he wanted to minimize. His sleight of hand would simply be performed in the editing room instead of onstage.

I began to think about the specific ways that the art of illusion is transferable to other fields and endeavors. Wouldn't we all like to control what others know and think about us? Don't we all *try* to highlight our successes and make our failures disappear? Don't those who *appear* to be several steps ahead of the competition usually wind up leading the pack?

Virtually all innovators, leaders, and CEOs push the boundaries of human experience and convince their audiences that the impossible is not only possible but necessary. They have plans and backup plans. They reverse-engineer. They read their surroundings with acute attention and capitalize on opportunities that others never notice. They implement unwavering command over the impression they leave on others. And that impression, when the illusion works, is one of respect and amazement.

THE WOW FACTOR

If the concept of the gap is central to the mechanics of illusion, the wow factor is the reason why illusion holds such power. To understand why, we again need look no further than human nature.

Just as we're wired to believe what we see, and to "see" with our minds more than our eyes can physically perceive, we're also preconditioned to sit up and take notice and, perhaps most important of all, to *remember* when we're surprised by something new. As humans, we love novelty. New dances. New inventions. New fashions. New flavors. Can you remember your first day of school? Your first flight in an airplane? Your first kiss? If so, you can thank the power of novelty. You remember the first experience not because it was intrinsically better or different than others that followed it but because it was totally new and different from anything that came before. In this sense, it surprised your expectations and made a deep impression.

During human beings' earliest developmental stages, experiences of surprise and puzzlement are integral to the learning process. One Johns Hopkins study of eleven-month-old infants explored the idea that babies learn best when they encounter events that "violate prior expectations." Cognitive psychologists Aimee Stahl and Lisa Feigenson presented babies with a number of simple illusions. One test group watched a ball roll down a ramp and pass through a seemingly solid wall. Then they were shown other, more ordinary, ways the ball moved. Another group watched a ball roll down the ramp and stop—predictably—at the wall, before being shown the same ball moves as the first group. The babies that had been surprised by the ball's behavior showed much more curiosity and learned more about the object. They experimented by banging, dropping, and rolling it like little scientists. In contrast, the group that had seen the ball behave predictably soon lost interest in it.

According to Feigenson, even the youngest infants form predictions about the world based on their prior observations and experiences. "When these predictions are shown to be wrong, infants use this as a special opportunity for learning."[9] Surprise, in other words, is a force for education.

Adults are no different. When an illusion delivers an amazing surprise, your audience remembers. But they don't just remember being surprised: They remember everything you told them; every detail you directed them to notice will also stay with them. The more surprising the effect, the more indelible the impression. And perhaps most important of all, the more *you* wow them, the larger you will loom for them as a superstar.

HOUDINI AND ROOSEVELT

No one managed the wow factor like Harry Houdini. After his first big break in 1899, when theater manager Martin Beck was mesmerized by his handcuff act, Houdini became known the world over as the ultimate escape artist. He could free himself from locked milk cans, buckled straitjackets while hanging from cranes, even submerged upside down in the "Chinese Water Torture Cell." Many of his admirers were convinced he must have superhuman powers to emerge alive from these traps.

SPELLBOUND

One of those admirers was President Theodore Roosevelt, who was in the audience in June 1914, aboard the SS *Imperator*, which was making its way to New York from Southampton, England. It was not a great escape that impressed the president, however, but Houdini's other "superhuman" ability: to mimic spiritualism.

During an evening show for the ship's passengers, Houdini asked his audience to submit questions to the "spirit slates" (miniature blackboards on which chalk writing would eerily appear). Roosevelt wrote on his slip of paper: "Where was I last Christmas?"

Houdini placed the president's challenge between the two blank slates. When he separated them, chalk images had appeared: on one slate a colored drawing of the map of Brazil; on the other, the words *Near the Andes*. Roosevelt was dumbfounded. Having been out of office for five years, he considered himself a private citizen now, and the details of this expedition had not been publicized.

The next day Roosevelt cornered the magician, asking "man to man" if spirits had really written on the slates.

"No, Colonel," Houdini replied. "It was just hocus-pocus."

Knowing that Roosevelt would be a fellow passenger, Houdini had prepared for this act before even boarding the ship. He'd turned to contacts at the *London Telegraph* to learn every secret he could about the ex-president, which is how he found out about the precise details of the South American expedition. Houdini had planned to have another audience member pose the question of Roosevelt's recent whereabouts, but the "Colonel's" own question instead played directly into his hands, allowing Houdini to pull one over on the Rough Rider himself.

"MIND CONTROL" AND MAJOR CONS

Unfortunately, some masters of illusion are also dangerous operators. The power that supposed sorcerers have wielded throughout history and around the globe is a testament to magic's dark side. According to semiotician Dawn Perlmutter, who analyzes the role of symbols in religious terrorism and ritualistic crimes, belief in witchcraft, ghosts, and demons still holds considerable global sway today. In the Muslim world, for example, this widespread belief is rooted in the concept of spirits known as jinn. "Jinn provide Islamic explanations for evil, illness, health, wealth, and position in society as well as all mundane and inexplicable phenomena in between. The word *jinn* (also written as *jinnee, djinn, djinni, genii* or *genie*) itself derives from the Arabic root j-n-n meaning to hide or be hidden, similar to the Latin origins of the word 'occult' (hidden)."[10] In other words, the power of jinn is intrinsically linked to these spirits' illusory nature.

While Islamic clerics typically denounce or prohibit magical practices that threaten their own religious authority, many secular leaders in Muslim countries exploit mysticism for their own political ends. Mullah Omar, the Pashtun founder of the Taliban, claimed to be magically protected by a cloak taken from a chest that supposedly could only be opened by a true leader. When Omar's forces took Kabul, credulous Afghans believed that his strength was supernatural. (They also believed that he was still alive two years after he'd died, in 2013, from tuberculosis.) Likewise, then–Iranian president Mahmoud Ahmadinejad announced in 2005 that he "was surrounded by a halo of light during a speech to the U.N. General Assembly, in which the foreign leaders in the hall were transfixed, unable to blink for a half hour."[11] In a *Wall Street Journal* interview, Iranian sorcerer Seyed Sadigh claimed that he routinely advises Iran's top government officials after consulting "jinn who can help out on matters of national security and the regime's political stability. His regular roll call includes jinn who work for . . . the Mossad, and for the U.S. Central Intelligence Agency."[12]

Closer to home, for more than seven years while Nancy Reagan was first lady, astrologer Joan Quigley guided her in scheduling the president's press conferences, speeches, flights of Air Force One, medical procedures, and even political debates.[13] And politicians of all stripes, according to political scientist Michael Curtis, exploit the fact that "people believe what they want to believe."[14]

"Success in politics," Curtis writes, "is like success at performing card tricks, with false shuffling of cards, but making sure the right one is always on top. If magicians skillfully deceive the viewer, politicians similarly engage in spin, misinformation or outright deception." Or, as Richard Nixon put it, "concern for image must rank with concern for substance."[15]

Magicians, politicians, and shysters alike play to explanations and impressions that the public *wants* to believe. Ahmadinejad, Sadigh, and Mullah Omar were well versed in the jinn that their audiences feared and revered. Quigley knew just how much Nancy Reagan *wanted* to trust in astrology. And American politicians of all political stripes know how badly voters want to trust in quick and simple solutions. That's why, Curtis says, "[c]omplex and countless controversial issues, such as cap and trade, the flat tax, migration, Medicaid, budget deficit, Obamacare, tax limits and cuts, deductions for home mortgages, and U.S. policy in Syria, are reduced to a simple prescription."

Mentalists, magicians who pretend to read your mind, know just what their audiences want to believe. Using the very same tools as other illusionists, they claim to have telepathic or paranormal powers, such as the ability to communicate with your dear, departed aunt Sophie. YouTube features a number of videos, some of them demonstrative pranks, in which "psychics" approach bystanders and "divine" information about them. The videos then reveal that these marks had, just minutes earlier, shared their name and location to an app such as Instagram. This information served as the virtual trailhead from which the illusionist could google his way to the details he'd used to wow his gullible target.

Mentalists ruffle the feathers of the rest of the magic community because they pretend they were born with mind-reading gifts. Most magicians generally restrict their illusions to the stage and their purposes to entertainment, but mentalists, and their more predatory counterparts, psychics and fortune-tellers, keep their supernatural acts going 24/7. Worse, they righteously deny any and all illusion or chicanery as the modus operandi for their clairvoyant abilities. Even within magic circles, I've seen mentalists shift uncomfortably when they are complimented for their sleight of hand or clever use of gimmicks, worried that their act will be exposed.

Ever since the beginning of modern spiritualism in 1848, when the Fox sisters claimed to hear spirits "rapping" in their home in Hydesville, New York, there have been magicians who sought to expose such fraud. In 1876, John Nevil Maskelyne testified against Henry Slade, a slate-medium (a spiritualist who received ghostly messages on writing slates), demonstrating in court how Slade's trick table actually worked.

Houdini, too, crusaded against fake mediums who fleeced grieving patrons while "communicating" with their lost loved ones. He would attend séances in disguise, accompanied by a reporter and policeman, who'd arrest the frauds after the magician revealed their tricks. In 1924, Houdini published *A Magician Among the Spirits*, giving detailed descriptions of techniques for slate writing, table rapping, levitation, and spirit manifestations. He was so incensed by spiritualism's insidious use of illusion that he testified in Congress in 1926 on behalf of a bill to outlaw fortune-telling in the District of Columbia. "I have had more mediums arrested in two years than have been arrested in seventy," he said, "because I know their tricks. I know how to catch them." Mastery of the principles of illusion, in other words, is the best defense against masters of deception.[16]

In 2015, the storied career of magician and psychic debunker James Randi was featured in the documentary *An Honest Liar*. The title of the film is perhaps the most apt description of an illusionist's credo. As Randi himself puts it in the film's opening scene: "Magicians are the most honest people in the world. They tell you they're going to fool you, and then they do it." It's understood by both magician and audience that his use of subterfuge is purely for their entertainment.

On the complete opposite end of the spectrum we have faith healer Peter Popoff, who in 1986 was earning about $4 million a year as a televangelist with supposedly divine powers. At his massive revival meetings, Popoff would call out to individual members of the audience as if divinely informed of their name and specific affliction. Randi, who was determined to expose the con, found that the faith healer's wife was feeding him these "miraculous" insights through his wireless earpiece. Another Popoff tactic involved providing courtesy wheelchairs to audience members who didn't need them. When Popoff "cured" their supposed infirmities, they'd discard the wheelchairs and amaze the rest of the audience by walking back to their seats.

After Randi exposed Popoff on *The Tonight Show* in 1986, he thought he'd scored a major victory, and the minister did later declare bankruptcy. Unfortunately, people still believe what they want to believe. And what many *most* want to believe is that there's a way to access some higher power that can heal, rescue, or restore them. Having spent years studying his followers' fears and desires, Popoff wasn't about to surrender. He knew he still had a willing captive audience, and by 1998 he was purchasing airtime on faith-based cable networks and making infomercials for the very same "healing abilities" that Randi had debunked. In 2005, his ministry took in more than $23 million.[17] The following year the Peter Popoff Ministries filed as a church instead of a for-profit business, thus relieving the operation of both taxes and public financial records.

Today Popoff's real profit machine is his mail campaign. You can send in a prayer request and hope to hear back from the ministry with instructions on how to carry out "supernatural debt cancellation." You'll receive a small container of "miracle spring water," to be sprinkled over your debt-ridden property. It won't work, however, unless you "give God a sacrificial offering. Give your biggest bill (or check)."[18] Ole Anthony, who tracks religious fraud as president of the public nonprofit Trinity Foundation, has found that most televangelists "are fooled by their own theology. . . . But in the case of Popoff, 'He's fundamentally evil. Because he knows he's a con man.'"[19]

Of course, you don't have to invoke mystical powers to turn illusion into a con game. Bernie Madoff's Ponzi scheme is perhaps the most spectacular recent example of a secular con. As one of the most influential people in finance, Madoff commanded the unwavering respect of Wall Street. The wealth management division of his investment firm attracted major philanthropic institutions, hospitals, colleges, international banks and funds, family trusts, and celebrities, like Kevin Bacon, Eric Roth, John Malkovich, Zsa Zsa Gabor, and Larry King. All believed Madoff to be a financial wizard who could deliver stratospheric returns on their investments. In fact, Madoff was running the largest Ponzi scheme in history, funneling billions of dollars of investors' funds into fabricated gains.

Madoff's operation was what con experts call an "affinity scam," meaning that he preyed on people who shared his background. As a Jewish-American, Madoff lured affluent clients in New York, Palm Beach, Florida, and Greenwich, Connecticut. He'd spent his whole life studying their habits, tastes, and weaknesses, so he knew just how to win their trust—and appeal to their core desires. Madoff's promised results were patently too good to be true, but that's not what his victims wanted to believe. Like a faith healer or fortune-teller, he was able to make his marks feel that they were part of an elite and exceptionally lucky group of winners. As Maria Konnikova writes in her book *The Confidence Game: Why We Fall For It . . . Every Time*, "that's the power of the good con artist: the ability to identify your deepest need and exploit it. It's not about honesty or greed; we are all suckers for belief."[20]

In 1999, a financial analyst named Harry Markopolos took just five minutes to realize that the returns Madoff promised were mathematically impossible to achieve. As an objective observer, he wasn't alone. "Hundreds of people suspected something was amiss," Markopolos told *60 Minutes*. "If you look at who the victims were not, you'll notice that the major firms on Wall Street had no money with Mr. Madoff." Yet Madoff knew his fellow investors well enough to know they'd never dare try to bring him down. "Because people in glass houses don't throw stones."[21]

Markopolos alerted the Securities and Exchange Commission five times between 2000 and 2008, but it wasn't until 2008 that Madoff was finally arrested and charged. All told, the scam involved a fraud of more than $50 billion.

Peter Popoff and Bernie Madoff were con artists who preyed on the public's appetite for illusion. But what happens when that insatiable appetite itself starts calling the shots? The ongoing saga of Theranos Inc. may offer a cautionary tale. In 2014 Elizabeth Holmes's diagnostic laboratories company was Silicon Valley's prized unicorn for its advances in microfluidic technology. Theranos's handheld blood-testing device, named Edison, was supposed to be able to furnish lab results from just a few drops of blood drawn from the finger. The promise of cheap, simple, painless blood tests resulted in a massive deal with Walgreens, enabling Holmes's company unparalleled accessibility and credibility to consumers. Investors dumped more than $400 million into Theranos, resulting in a company valuation of $9 billion. But in 2015 the company came under fire for inaccurate test results. Walgreens and other pharmacies pulled the plug on their deals to build blood-draw centers for

Theranos. In 2016, federal regulators barred Holmes from owning or operating a medical laboratory. According to *Forbes*, her net worth dropped from $4.5 billion to nil.

Business blogger Mark St. Cyr described Theranos's corporate strategy: "Build something that can give the illusion VC's want to see and hear so they can pay for the right to then sell that illusion to Wall Street and we all get rich."[22] With such eagerness to alchemize hype into VC gold, the temptation to package outright lies as promises may be understandable, but that doesn't make this practice justifiable—or wise.

Aryeh Bourkoff, founder and CEO of boutique investment bank LionTree LLC, is no stranger to Wall Street wealth. In 2015, he brokered the sale of Time Warner Cable to Charter Communications for $56 billion. Nor does he deny the potency of illusion in capitalism. "Creating an illusion in business," he told me, "is creating value where it seemingly didn't exist before." However, Bourkoff sees no role for underhanded practices in this equation. "If you create an 'outside the box' approach, but still play *by the ethical rules of the game*, meaning you don't lie, then you have the best chance of getting the best and impactful results." You can't violate or change the basic rules of the game, he says. Otherwise things won't be fair. The common goal must be to "add value. The pie has to grow." And what makes the pie grow, in Bourkoff's estimation, is trust. "Trust with the client is the key to all of this and must be cherished and held sacred."

The moral of all these stories is that illusions are powerful tools of persuasion. But they can be used for good, or for evil; to strengthen systems, or to subvert them; to lead, or to deceive. Be careful what you wish for, and be careful how you handle the wishes of others.

⟶   **MIND THE GAP**

2

LOAD UP

The Human Card Index was a vaudevillian magician named Arthur Lloyd, who began performing on the American stage in 1917. Lloyd could turn water into wine, make a broken plate whole, or make a live duck appear inside a previously empty pan. But his specialty was a trick that no one else to this day has matched—or ever fully figured out.

By 1925, Lloyd was challenging his audiences to "name a card, any card." He wore a university gown (of the cap-and-gown variety) that was lined with dozens of pockets, each one loaded with a selection of business cards, calling cards, playing or bingo cards, membership or menu cards, and more. In fact, Lloyd could produce virtually anything on paper that his audience called for, from lottery and meal tickets to marriage licenses, memos to claim checks, divorce papers to war bonds, ration coupons to bankbooks, boxing licenses to playbills. So frequently did someone yell out "shirt card," that Lloyd was prepared for this as well. As a climax to the routine, Lloyd would unbutton his shirt and produce a large piece of shirt cardboard.[1] In 1936, Ripley's *Believe It or Not* announced that his fully loaded gown weighed 45 pounds and concealed 15,000 items.

Somehow, Lloyd almost always had the very card requested, *and* he knew precisely where to reach for it. Whatever the intricacies of his preparations, they made it possible for him to stay at least one step ahead of his audience. (On the extremely rare occasions when he *couldn't* meet a challenge, he'd jot down the particulars and make sure to pocket it before he returned for his next engagement in that city.)

Lloyd's very public specialty was a practice that most magicians perform in secret. Called "loading up," it involves the advance organization and placement of devices that will later be used to create a magical effect. Illusionists, close-up magicians in particular, might load up by running strings up and down their coat sleeves, or stuffing their pockets with gimmicked coins, extra cards, or maybe a fake thumb or sixth finger. Whatever equipment is called for, it will be loaded precisely so that it can be accessed and deployed the instant it's needed, but without the audience's knowledge—inside the gap, so to speak, between what they can see and what they will perceive. What they'll perceive, of course, is the seemingly spontaneous effect: the payoff of all these preparations.

While magicians generally use the term *load up* only when referring to the rigging of devices or placement of hidden objects before a trick is executed, the broader principle includes preliminary planning and mental strategy, as well as physical preparation and practice. I'm not talking about doing your assigned homework or "being prepared" in the Boy Scout sense. What distinguishes an illusionist's approach to preparation are the extreme lengths to which he or she will go to ensure a desired outcome. Master illusionist David Copperfield, for example, is known to take two years to develop a piece that requires only minutes to perform, and especially complicated tricks can take even longer. One of his most famous acts, "Flying," in which he soared around the stage, passing through hoops and a Plexiglas box, took him seven years to perfect.

Of course, magic has no corner on the need for preparation. Many other businesses require equally rigorous planning and organization. Rosabeth Moss Kanter directs the Harvard Advanced Leadership Initiative at Harvard Business School. As Kanter puts it, "Instant success takes time." For her book *Confidence*, Kanter conducted an investigation of success and failure in companies like Continental Airlines and Verizon, and sports teams such as the New England Patriots and Philadelphia Eagles, as well as in the arenas of education, health care, and politics. She found that, quite simply, perpetual winners tend to work harder than long-term losers. "Winners are more likely to take the time to keep honing skills and testing ideas in preparation for change. That's not too dramatic or glamorous, but it's among the biggest differentiators."[2]

In the restaurant industry, the practice of preparation is so crucial that it approaches an art in itself. If you've ever watched *Top Chef* or any of its competitors, you probably know the phrase *mise en place*—the equivalent of "loading up" in the culinary world. *Mise en place* is French for "put in place," and it refers to the exacting method by which ingredients and tools are selected, organized, and prepared for use in every professional kitchen. *Mise en place* is a foundational principle in the restaurant industry, just as loading up is in magic, because it puts the performer steps ahead of the audience and, in so doing, makes the ultimate effect *seem* magical.

Cooks may do six hours of prep for a three-hour dinner shift, but that preparation allows kitchen crews to keep up with orders when it counts. Meal service time in a restaurant is the equivalent of stage time during a magic show. And according to Manhattan chef and restaurant owner Bill Telepan, not a second can be wasted. "The one minute behind you are now is going to become six minutes behind" if you have to scramble to catch up or fix a mistake when other orders are lined up and customers are waiting.[3] His rule is to slow down *in advance*, to get ready and make certain that everything he needs is in place. This allows him to speed up and stay ahead of demand when it matters most.

This process of preparation applies to all fields of endeavor, not just cooking. Chef Dwayne LiPuma, who teaches at the Culinary Institute of America, explains, "By being organized, you will be more efficient. By being more efficient, you will have more time in your day. By having more time in your day, you will be more relaxed in your day; you will be able to accomplish the task at hand in a clear, concise, fluid motion." Smooth and controlled. Like magic.

"You *mise-en-place* your life," one of LiPuma's students told a reporter in 2014. "You set up your books for class, you set up your chef whites, your shoes are shined, you know everything that you need every step of the day." In other words, you load up for success.

STEPPING AHEAD

Several years ago, at a retreat for superagency William Morris Endeavor, I capped a card trick by "spelling out" co-CEO Ari Emanuel's cell phone number. "How the fuck did you get that?" he shouted. "*Nobody* has that one." But I'd found a way, and the lengths to which I went have been rewarded ever since with invitations from WME partner Adam Venit to perform several times a year for his major clients. You can bet I prepare for those performances just as diligently as I did for the first, because each newly amazed audience helps to propel my career forward.

Staying at least one step ahead of the spectator is a fundamental rule throughout the practice of magic, but it's the whole point of loading up. You never show your hand up front. *You'll* know which effects matter most to you, but you won't reveal to others what they are, how much they matter, or why. Instead, you'll prepare discreetly and to such an extreme that you're ready for any and all contingencies. After all this secret front-loading, the advantage is resoundingly yours, but *no one else will know that*. And once you've pulled off your grand feat, they won't be able to figure out how you did it. They'll just think you're superhuman.

Lew Horwitz, an entertainment industry banker who also practices magic, leveraged this concept into incredible success back in the 1970s. At the time, the big studios mostly financed their own projects, and banks viewed independent producers as poor credit risks, so there was very little entertainment lending. But a couple of Horwitz's friends introduced him to a young actress who was trying to get a TV series off the ground for CBS, and although the other banks weren't interested, he thought it looked promising.

The obstacle was his own loan committee. They didn't want to be on the hook if the producers didn't complete their episodes. But as a magician, Horwitz knew the importance of loading up in advance to keep a step ahead. "So, I said, I have an idea. It's the one-ahead method. I'm going to use this for contracts!"

The one-ahead method, or principle, is a technique used by mentalists to glean information just moments in advance, then deploy it in a way that makes them appear clairvoyant. Here's a basic trick to illustrate how it works:

$\longrightarrow$ **LOAD UP**

1. You spread the cards in front of you but secretly glimpse and memorize the bottom card, the three of diamonds. You are "one ahead" with this one card.

2. You then touch the back of another card and "sense" its value, declaring, "This is the three of diamonds!" You look at the card to "verify" your claim, and announce, "Yes, I am correct!" However, *you do not show this card to the audience yet*, since it's actually the queen of spades. Instead, you say, "I will now sense the queen of spades!"

3. You pick up a new card. "Yes, correct again!" you announce as you alone look and see that it's actually the seven of hearts. "And last," you say, "I will pick up the seven of hearts!"

4. Now you pick up that bottom card—your original one-ahead card, which you remember is the three of diamonds.

5. Your grand finale is to remind the audience of the cards that you "predicted," and—finally—fan the cards for them to see for themselves that, indeed, all three of the cards you just named are in your hand.

The idea is to start off "one ahead" and then cleverly catch up to that secret in a way that disguises your advantage. Lew Horwitz realized that his "one ahead" was a value that he didn't yet have in hand, but knew was coming: the reimbursement that the producers were *already* promised by CBS.

The producers initially had paid $125,000 of their own money to create their pilot, and the studio was set to pay them back upon delivery. Lew proposed that, instead, the producers assign the payment to his bank in exchange for the new loan. This way, the studio's $125,000 would put the lender one step ahead of the customer—and create what essentially was a risk-free loan.

Horwitz's magic changed the whole field of entertainment financing. And that show that he made possible? *The Mary Tyler Moore Show.*

THE START IS HALF THE DEED

Dimidium facti qui coepit habet. No, that isn't a secret incantation. It's the wisdom of Horace from 20 BC, and it translates as: He who has begun has half done. "Dare to be wise," the Roman knight-poet added. "Begin!"

All this to say that getting ready to do something great isn't always easy, but it is more important than you might realize. Smart leaders, like magicians, know there's a science to preparation, which has to do with how we learn and train to perform.

First, preparation is a whole-body endeavor. When we first begin to think about doing or learning something brand-new, we are like neurological virgins; we have no specific circuits in the brain that are ready to execute the skill. However, we do have other skill-related circuits that can be enlisted to jump-start the effort. The motor cortex, as the region of the brain that maps all physical movement, directs those enlisted circuits to get busy creating new neurons and sending them to the muscles where they're needed.

Let's say you're learning to ski. You'll train your brain to create this new neural network by spending hours on the slopes, starting with the bunny hill and working your way up to the diamonds. During this activity, your motor cortex will send signals to all the necessary muscles to focus, flex, lean, snowplow, and traverse. It won't be instantaneous, but eventually, the neurons in the muscles will obey the message. Then, with more practice, they'll remember it—that's muscle memory—so that the movements will happen naturally. With a lot of practice, your moves on the slopes will become reflexive, almost automatic. That's when the skill is internalized. Your muscles no longer require your conscious direction, because the neurological signals are traveling down such well-established paths—as if they themselves are skiing.

This neurological process explains why practice really does eventually make perfect, not just in physical skills, but in the mastery of illusion as well. The more expertise your brain has frontloaded, the more steps ahead you're likely to be.

This was my epiphany in the fall of 2010, as I struggled to come up with a large-scale trick to perform at the Magic Castle in Los Angeles. This private club's membership consists exclusively of professional magicians and associates who support the art of magic. Over the years I'd given many impromptu shows for small groups huddled around tables in dimly lit corners of the sprawling mansion. But this time I wanted to throw a party and showcase something for a larger, more serious crowd.

The problem was, none of my tricks seemed bold enough. If only I had the expertise of renowned illusion designer Jim Steinmeyer or of the younger crop of trick engineers like Francis Menotti and Calen Morelli . . . But then it dawned on me: I have an area of my own expertise that's unique in magic—I construct crossword puzzles! If I could figure out a way to cross-pollinate my skills in puzzles with my ability in magic, I'd create a whole new type of illusion.

In the process, I'd be capitalizing on twenty years of crossword puzzle practice that had loaded me up with highly specialized brain circuitry. I'd already wired myself for puzzles and, separately, for performing illusions. Now I just needed to join the two circuits, and I'd be primed to create a new hybrid skill. When surfers in the 1940s began putting roller-skate wheels on wooden boards, they must have felt a similar thrill.

My idea was to create the illusion of spontaneous puzzle construction—writing a *New York Times* crossword on the fly. I just had to have every possible permutation of the grid under control, or at least within reach.

I began drafting crossword grid after crossword grid. Like a magician loaded up with mechanisms to allow him to improvise magic, I would have word and letter patterns at my fingertips. Like Arthur Lloyd, I'd challenge my audience to "name a word, *any* word!" Then, using their prompts, I'd construct a grid that "worked" by varying the positions of the black squares and the surrounding "fill" words.

I practiced with hundreds of index cards laid out on my kitchen table. For the most part, I drew pictures on the cards to help me remember word combinations. If the word ANTARCTICA necessitated surrounding words SOMBRERO, COUSIN, and BARLEY, I would sketch a picture of my cousin Daniel, holding a sombrero full of barley, standing on a glacier. For months I was never without flashcards, often drilling myself while stuck in Los Angeles traffic.

⟶ **LOAD UP**

MEMORY METHODS

Magicians and memory specialists have a long intertwined history together. Mentalists are known to memorize the contents of a random magazine, a list of items generated by the audience, or a shuffled pack of playing cards.

"Mathemagician" Arthur Benjamin is renowned for his original methods of rapid mental calculation. For the astounding finale of his show, Benjamin squares any audience-suggested four-digit number. The result is a solution in the millions or tens of millions. In order to accomplish this feat, Benjamin utilizes the Major System, a technique for converting numbers into words. If he has to hold on to the digits 684, for example, he'll convert it into a word and come back to it later. In the Major System, 6 is "ch as in cheese, sh, or a soft g"; 8 is "f, ph, or v"; and 4 is "r." Why memorize three numbers when you can convert it into the word SHIVER? Likewise, 735, composed of 7 ("k, or hard c"), 3 ("m"), and 5 ("l"), can be thought of as CAMEL.

Memory methods typically engage multiple types of memory—semantic, numerical, ordinal, visual—to work together to make information multifaceted and, ideally, unforgettable. This is the underlying principle found in *The Memory Book*, the classic treatise on improving memory by Harry Lorayne. Born in 1926, Lorayne is rightfully revered by magicians for his decades of writing about and teaching sleight of hand. But Lorayne was most famous for his memory feats. As a regular guest on *The Tonight Show* with Johnny Carson, he would memorize the names of hundreds of audience members.

SPELLBOUND

One memory method that Lorayne teaches in his books is the Peg System. If you have to memorize a list of suggested items in order, correlate each item with a visual noun that rhymes with the number of its position. Commonly, 1 = gun, 2 = shoe, 3 = tree, and 4 = door. Then picture the item with its ordinal clue. If the suggested items were *cell phone, peanut butter, alligator,* and *candle,* you might visualize a cell phone being fired from a gun, a shoe filled with peanut butter, an alligator climbing a tree, and a door with a candle painted on it.

On the night of the party, I stood in front of the room and performed a number of card tricks to warm up the crowd. The last of these finished with me failing to produce the jack of hearts, so I promised the audience I would come back to this card later. Then I turned to the large board behind me, a grid of 15x15 squares, the dimensions of the daily *New York Times* crossword. On a side table were various shapes of black squares—single squares, bars, and L shapes—to be placed in the grid to break up unfavorable letter combinations.

I asked the audience to name a U.S. state. Someone yelled "Massachusetts," which, fortunately, has an odd number of letters. This allowed me to place it in the center of the grid. Then I went to work, alternately blacking in sections around it and spelling out words to the corners of the grid. Along the way, to constrain my freedom, I asked for prompts of letters and words, each of which I entered into the puzzle. When I scrawled the last letter into the final square the audience cheered.

⟶   **LOAD UP**

But then I paused. There was one more thing. Did the audience remember that playing card I'd failed to produce earlier? I circled the letters that formed a diagonal of the grid. J-A-C-K-O-F-H-E-A-R-T-S.

That "kicker" elicited a roar from the crowd that will never be rivaled in my career. I was playing at the Magic Castle, after all, to an audience of my peers, and every magician in the room knew that I had created something entirely new. It would go on to become my signature trick, one I'd perform at Google, Amazon, eBay, design conventions, and the TED conference. My career hasn't slowed down since.

The success of this trick got me thinking about the reasons why audiences are so wildly receptive to breakthrough achievements. I realized that one reason we applaud innovation is that we all appreciate how difficult it is to be *proactive*, to imagine the future and initiate change—to jump the gap from theory to proof.

Many of us spend much of our lives *reacting* to situations that we feel are beyond our control. Those who excel in work and in life, however, tend to excel at being proactive.

As in: The best defense is a good offense.

CALIBRATE YOUR ENDGAME

Whether you call it *mise en place* or loading up for success, the process of proactivity starts with envisioning the effect you ultimately want to achieve. The perfectly cooked and plated meal? A can't-lose business deal, or the magical illusion that will launch your career? The more important your objective is to you, the more important it is that you load up carefully. There's no reason to stress over routine events. But when you approach an important career hurdle, a once-in-a-lifetime chance, the Olympics of your life—solid preparation will ensure that you perform with absolute confidence.

For me, those important pursuits include all the illusions I perform publicly. I actually go to such extremes of preparation that my acts sometimes fool other magicians, who can't imagine that I'd prepare more than *they* do. However, I'm a piker when compared to the legendary greats.

John Mulholland, one of the leading prestidigitators of the twentieth century, literally wrote the book on preparation for magic tricks, and the story of this book itself illustrates the importance of knowing—and concealing—your endgame as you load up. For this was no ordinary magic manual.

In 1953, at the height of the Cold War, Mulholland was approached by Sidney Gottlieb, head of the CIA's top secret "Project MKUltra," a program involving the covert use of drugs and chemicals to influence, incapacitate, discredit, or "eliminate" enemy agents. Gottlieb wanted Mulholland to teach CIA operatives the tactics of illusion so that they could administer their chemicals in the field without being detected. The ethics and legality of Gottlieb's program are eminently debatable, but as Mulholland saw it, his job was to translate his deep understanding of magic into a manual that would help keep America safe. He accepted the challenge.

Mulholland was used to keeping secrets, but this time the stakes were higher than for any ordinary magic act. With American spies' lives on the line, he committed himself full-time to his mission. Citing "health concerns" he shuttered the *Sphinx*, the magic magazine that he'd edited for twenty-three years, and stepped out of the public eye. Still, fear of detection ran so high that the CIA created an elaborate ruse to conceal the magician's true work and paymaster even

———————→   **LOAD UP**

from the IRS. There was no written contract or other documentation of the magician's employment by the CIA. And the manual itself had to look like an ordinary magic book, with no reference to "agents," "operatives," "covert actions," or "poisons." Instead, Mulholland would address instructions to "performers," who executed "tricks" that involved "small objects."

The first step was to clarify the book's functions. Like any other magician, Mulholland needed a crystal clear and accurate vision of his endgame before he could design his methods to achieve it. But because his book actually would be a guide to loading up (for acts of espionage), the list that he compiled can be read as a key to preparation for any major undertaking:

1. Supplying . . . background facts in order that a complete novice in the subject can appreciate the underlying reasons for the procedures suggested. . . . In this section would be given alternative procedures . . . as well as changes in procedure needed as situations and circumstances vary.

2. Detailed descriptions of [techniques] . . . explanations of [the skills] required and how quickly to master such skills . . . adaptations and modifications of the best existing [methods] to fit new requirements.

3. A variety of examples to show in detail how to make use of the [techniques] previously described. These examples would be given with varying situations and the ways to accommodate procedure to meet variations.[4]

Mulholland's book had to prepare his future readers for all contingencies, so he needed to research every situation in which a spy might have to palm a vial of poison or misdirect an enemy's gaze. He had to envision all circumstances that might interfere with a "trick," and come up with response maneuvers. And in addition to writing out his instructions, he needed to diagram them so the steps could be visualized. The same general approach—minus the particulars of spycraft—would have served him equally well if he'd been preparing to launch a company or introduce a new product.

It took Mulholland nearly two years to complete his assignment, but the final results were so effective that the CIA hired him for another assignment, and then another. Because he'd trained himself for more than thirty years to be scrupulously thorough, dogged, and discreet in preparing for his own magic tricks, it was second nature to be just as meticulous in loading up for his CIA assignments.

Consider the goals that matter most in your career and personal life. Now ask yourself how you can best prepare to reach those objectives. What do you need to learn to put yourself at the top of your game? What skills will give you the greatest advantage? What could be added to your repertoire to help you jump the gap between your particular audience's expectations and your triumphal performance?

Maybe you need to research your next job interviewer and read all the books that have most influenced her. Perhaps you should study the history of your key client's favorite Scotch. Better yet, target an entirely new way to meet your audience's needs.

In 1985, Lorenzo Zambrano, CEO of the Mexican cement company Cemex, wanted to grow his profits. He investigated all his options and decided that his product was fine, but by changing the way he *delivered* that product he could gain a significant edge over the competition. Because mixed concrete has an extremely short shelf life, it has to be delivered right before the customer is ready to pour it. So Zambrano realized that instead of tinkering with the price per cubic yard, he'd be wise to load up on fresh ideas for refining his delivery methods and for keeping his concrete ready until the exact moment his customers called for it.

He started by quietly studying delivery methods in *other* industries. He had his staff research FedEx, pizza delivery companies, and trucking and ambulance services. What emerged were digital systems that could redirect Cemex trucks in real time and optimize routing across large service areas. If one customer had to postpone an order at the last minute, the delivery could instantly be rerouted to another who had just placed an urgent order. Customers were no longer penalized if circumstances forced them to change an order. Delivery time shrank. And Cemex grew from a regional company to one of the largest ready-mix concrete companies in the world.[5]

The preparation that paved the way for Zambrano's success was both exhaustive and surprising. He kept it secret for good reason. Those still operating under the old methods had no glimmer of the threat he posed—until he unleashed his new operations. And then he roared past them.

KNOW YOUR AUDIENCE

As the Cemex story shows, one vital aspect of preparation is audience research. Zambrano had to understand his customer's habits, problems, and needs before he could mastermind a system to win their business. But they weren't his only audience; he was also preparing to surpass his competitors, so he had to know their practices and assumptions—their culture—well enough to keep them in the dark, even as he was outsmarting them.

Another example. David Rockefeller, former chair of Chase Manhattan, kept a Rolodex with one hundred thousand names filed by name as well as geography. His contacts ranged from prime ministers to the doormen at prestigious hotels where he'd stayed throughout the world. But the cards contained more than addresses. Each one was loaded with notes about Rockefeller's past encounters with the person. There were cryptic details about business meetings, social encounters, family news, and favors exchanged—information that would ordinarily fall into the gap of oblivion.

Thanks to his system, Rockefeller could control that gap to create the illusion of both familiarity and personal interest in anyone with whom he had history. At one meeting he impressed the former president of Mexico, Miguel de la Madrid Hurtado, by smoothly recalling each of nine previous meetings the two men had had over the course of thirty years. The effect was to make de la Madrid feel important and valued even as he was wowed by Rockefeller's extraordinary command.[6]

Magicians, too, keep close track of their audiences. One reason is to safeguard the element of surprise. Ideally, no spectator should ever see the same trick twice. If they do, they'll likely think, Ha, I'll watch his *other* hand this time. That could put the illusion in jeopardy, and it definitely will drain the act of its wow factor for that individual. So magicians must remember who's seen each act before, and make sure to deliver something new if an audience returns.

To prevent repeat performances, I punch the following information into a spreadsheet after every show: the date, the venue, who was there, and what tricks I performed. I try to input every name I can recall. That way when I perform for the second year in a row at the Milken Conference, for example, I won't close with my Morse code trick again, but end with the Scrabble routine instead.

Caesars Palace in Las Vegas uses a bit more sophisticated system to track its audience. Repeat visitors are invited to join Caesars' Total Rewards loyalty program,[7] which starts capturing data as soon as a customer uses it to make a reservation. The Total Rewards number links to all activities in the hotel, including entertainment and gambling. Caesars learns each Rewards member's betting habits, what games she plays, what performers she likes, and what hours she keeps. The reception she receives the next time she calls for a reservation is tailored accordingly. If her data reveal a mysterious history of winning big—at the casino's expense, of course—she may be told all rooms are booked. However, if her baccarat game tends to profit Caesars and she's shown to be a big Mariah Carey fan, she could be invited back with free tickets the next time Carey plays Caesars.

The idea is to use your memory bank to help you develop the relationships that matter most to you, while safeguarding yourself against those that spell danger. But what if you're planning to meet an audience for the very first time? Well, sometimes loading up on information about your audience can look a lot like spying.

That's how legendary art dealer Joseph Duveen familiarized himself with his intended client Andrew Mellon. In the early 1900s the industrialist Mellon was one of the richest men *and* one of the foremost art collectors in the world. Duveen was determined to win him over, even though the two had never met. So Duveen studied Mellon. He purchased information from Mellon's servants. He learned his quarry's routines and peculiarities, what he liked and what he didn't, where he traveled, and where he stayed. Finally, in 1921, Duveen knew his audience well enough to approach him.

He booked himself into the same London hotel where Mellon was staying and "by chance" rode down with him in the elevator and "just happened" to be going to the National Gallery, as he knew Mellon was. The "coincidence" made it seem natural for the two men to stroll through the museum together, but what won Mellon over was Duveen's "uncanny" knowledge about the very same works of art that most excited *him*. How was it possible that the two of them had such similar taste?

When he returned to New York, Mellon visited Duveen's gallery and was awestruck by the collection he found there, which seemed almost magically assembled to please him. The magnate became Duveen's best customer and remained loyal to him for the rest of his life.[8]

In magic, too, nothing stuns "random" volunteers more than when an illusionist mentions personal details that he, a total stranger, should have no way of knowing. Unlike Duveen, however, today's magicians use Facebook. And Google, Tinder, Twitter, Instagram, YouTube, LinkedIn, Match, MySpace, Pinterest, Tumblr . . . For all the concern in the media about privacy, most people freely release much more data out into the world than they realize or remember. Those handy apps in your smartphones and tablets are actually little broadcast networks that beam to the world at large your up-to-the-minute location, your habits and preferences, spending history, interests, friends, education, professional contacts, political persuasions, and pet fancies.

The lesson here is neither to become paranoid, nor to use other people's information maliciously or illegally. But if you want to command your audiences, by all means, use every legitimate tool at your disposal. Research your potential employer or employee, clients, colleagues, or interviewer. Prepare yourself for a blind date by loading up on information about this stranger—and not just from OkCupid or the friend who's set you up. Deep data is power—as more and more businesses are proving.

Companies have long used customer relationship management (CRM) software to track and measure information across departments, services, and phases of customer interaction. A retail chain might use CRM software, say, to create surveys and compare the results with data from sales and customer relations departments in order to learn which ads or marketing campaigns were most successful. But now, in the era of Big Data and the Internet of Things, CRM software seems almost quaint.

Today's corporate approach to loading up is to plug and play and mix and match every available technology, to learn as much real-time information as possible about individual customer behavior, then use that data immediately to improve the customer's experience as it's happening.

Disney's MyMagic+ system allows Walt Disney World Resort guests to plan their trips through an app called My Disney Experience. This helps Disney load up information about them in advance. Then, when they arrive at the resort, they're given a MagicBand bracelet that allows them to skip long lines and access extras, such as souvenir photographs, more easily. The bands report where their wearers are in real time, so Disney can text the guests' smartphones suggesting routes to get around congestion, or nearby places to find a cold drink.[9]

SPELLBOUND

By better understanding the needs and patterns of visitors, Disney can enhance their experience, which should solidify their brand loyalty and keep them coming back for more. The collective data from MyMagic+ also amounts to a megaload of information that Disney can use in planning improvements to the parks. In truth, Disney has more to gain than guests do from MyMagic+, but the illusion is that the guest reaps all the rewards. That illusion has to be maintained, or else no one would volunteer to be tracked and monitored.

So be judicious in deploying the data you've secretly loaded up. Mind the gap between what your audience thinks you know and what you actually know, and use your insights to awe them, but try not to reveal anything that might compromise your advantage.

THE EISENHOWER MATRIX

President Dwight D. Eisenhower famously said, "I have two kinds of problems, the urgent and the important. The urgent are not important, and the important are never urgent." This is a useful insight to keep in mind when getting ready to attack a new project or goal. Even after you've clarified your objectives and loaded up on information about your audience, the next steps can seem overwhelming.

Inspired by Eisenhower's quote is a handy time management tool that is named for him: the Eisenhower Matrix (or Eisenhower Box):

The Eisenhower Matrix clears through the focal clutter that makes it difficult to prioritize and organize the tasks that matter most. It helped President Eisenhower get past the clamor of people who insisted they urgently needed his attention, to decide what truly required his time and energy.

In 2014, Mary Burtzloff, archivist at the Eisenhower Presidential Library, offered some examples to illustrate his selection process:[10]

Urgent and Important: Sending in parts of the 101st Airborne Division to protect students under attack during the first efforts to integrate Little Rock Central High School in 1957.

Urgent but Not Important: The decision of whether or not to maintain the tradition of wearing a top hat to his Inauguration in 1953. (He did.)

Important but Not Urgent: The creation of the Federal Highway Act, which Eisenhower first saw as a necessity back in 1916 and which he finally signed into law in 1956.

Not Urgent and Not Important: Responding to the tens of thousands of personal notes that citizens sent to the White House, the vast majority of which could best be handled by staffers.

SPELLBOUND

The secret to using the Eisenhower Matrix is to remember Eisenhower's motto about urgency and importance. The important stuff needs to come first, even if there's no deadline attached to it. A lot of the demands on your time that seem urgent are simply a waste of your time. And, by all means, if a task can and should be handled by someone else, delegate!

GET ORGANIZED

Once you're clear on your target audience and priorities, the next step is to create a timeline. Productivity guru David Allen recommends listing each task with a verb to help remind you what you actually need to *do*. For example, instead of simply listing "Monday's presentation," you'd break down the actions required within a timetable:

- *Collect* sales figures by Wednesday, 5 p.m.
- *Draft* slides by Friday, 9 a.m.
- *Incorporate* images into deck by Monday, 9 a.m.
- *Deliver* presentation, Monday, 4 p.m.

Ron Friedman, author of *The Best Place to Work: The Art and Science of Creating an Extraordinary Workplace*, says that this advance mapping process helps to "minimize complex thinking later in the day and make procrastination less likely."[11] He also recommends organizing your timetable to place the most challenging tasks early in the day. "By starting each morning with a mini-planning session, you frontload important decisions to a time when your mind is fresh. You'll also notice that having a list of concrete action items (rather than a broad list of goals) is especially valuable later in the day, when fatigue sets in and complex thinking is harder to achieve. Now, no longer do you have to pause and think through each step." Instead, like a magician, you'll be able to devote your full attention to the execution of your plan.

If you really want to prepare like a magician, however, you'll first need to internalize that plan. When I'm in the final stages of getting ready for a show, I shouldn't have to stop to refer to my list of moves, and by the time I step onstage, I'd better know them cold. That's the ultimate goal of all this preparation, remember? To perform so naturally, so fluidly that your accomplishments occur as if by magic.

Wylie Dufresne, who won the James Beard Foundation's Best NYC Chef title in 2013, actually has a system for this internalization. "Let's say I had twenty-three items of *mise-en-place* I had to do every day. So I'd take a pad and I'd write them all down on the way home. And then I would crumple the list up and throw it out." Then on his way to work the next day, he'd write the list again. And destroy it again. "You become one with your list. You and the list are the same, because the list is scorched into your head."[12]

SET THE "STAGE"

Anthony Bourdain wrote in *Kitchen Confidential*, "As a cook, your station, and its condition, its state of readiness, is an extension of your nervous system. . . . The universe is in order when your station is set. . . ."

I feel the same way about setting up the stage before a show. *Know your angles* is one of the golden rules of my profession. The idea, intended to protect the magician's secret methods and techniques, is to know in advance exactly what people will be able to see and how they'll perceive it during the performance. Advance reconnaissance of the premises is essential if you're to know your angles.

When I prep the stage a few hours before a show, I'll take a seat in the first row on the aisle to see if the audience member who sits there will be able to glimpse what's happening in the wings. Then I'll move to the back of the house to check if I can see over the top of my prop case when it's onstage. I'll check the volume of the audio system and adjust it as necessary to mask the clinking of coins. And if I performed large-scale illusions, I'd tweak the lighting until all trace of thin wires, from the audience's perspective, just *vanished*.

The importance of setting the stage properly, however, is not limited to theatrical performance arenas. A 2014 study of kids in urban middle schools offered stark proof that stage setting can make a huge difference in education. Some of this preparation was environmental. At Philadelphia's John Paul Jones Middle School, the security bars were removed from the windows and the metal detectors were taken away, and without these constant physical reminders of danger, violence actually dropped—by a staggering 90 percent. Other forms of preparation involved the way lessons and activities were structured and how the very first assignments of the year were framed. The psychologists who conducted this study referred to such preparation as "setting the stage for thought and action," or "psychological *mise en place*."[13]

———————→   **LOAD UP**

The most astonishing research followed two groups of inner-city African-American seventh graders. At the start of the year, one group was given a brief series of assignments to write about "an important personal value." This value could involve relationships or personal passions, anything that was uniquely important to the student—in other words, that would engage him or her to behave proactively. The researchers called these "affirmational assignments," and the students who received them just a couple of times had higher grade point averages at the end of the term than the control group, whose assignments had been to write about neutral topics, such as their morning routine. The lowest-achieving students benefited most from the affirmational assignments; they saw almost a half-point rise in their GPA. But the kicker is that the benefits *continued*. These students were 13 percent less likely to be kept back a grade, and they were still doing better in school *two years* later.[14]

Those kids weren't necessarily what journalist Dan Charnas had in mind when he referred to *mise en place* as "a system that comes from the inside out . . . a system of personal improvement, not about efficiency, but about excellence."[15] But they certainly prove his point.

The bottom line, whether your stage is a kitchen or a proscenium, a classroom or a boardroom, is that every step of preparation is important when you expect to conduct important business. Remember: Magicians will spend hundreds of hours on a move that transpires in two seconds, because it's worth it to us. Once you've identified a goal that's worth your best effort, load up radically and stealthily in ways that no one else can imagine. Your moment will come. And when it does, all the care you've put into your preparation will make the accomplishment appear effortless—and you will look like a genius.

SPELLBOUND

3

WRITE THE SCRIPT

I n early 2014, Hollywood director Edgar Wright invited me to his home to teach him "how a magician thinks." Wright is known for his offbeat films: *Shaun of the Dead*, *Hot Fuzz*, *The World's End*, and *Scott Pilgrim vs. the World*. His equally offbeat friends include former bank robbers and confidence game experts—as well as magicians like me—so I wasn't particularly surprised when he requested a lesson in illusion, but I did take it as a special sort of challenge.

I invited my magician pal Blake Vogt to help me load up. Blake, in my opinion, is the best trick creator working today. A talented magician with an engineering background, he's often hired by marquee illusionists like David Blaine and Dynamo to create groundbreaking magic for their television specials.

Now, I'm going to tell you a secret: Magic without a strong story is like cake without sugar. Story is the ingredient that hooks and satisfies audiences emotionally. It draws them in, holds their attention, and makes them feel personally invested in the outcome of the experience that they're vicariously sharing with the performer.

So what Blake and I primarily engineered was the story that shaped Wright's magic lesson.

This story began with our arriving fifteen minutes behind schedule. We apologized profusely for not being able to find the house. Then we launched into a demonstration of an array of sleight-of-hand tricks in Wright's living room. Our lateness was forgiven. We chatted for a bit about the parallels and distinctions between magical deception and con artistry, and began wrapping up. All part of our script.

Then Edgar asked for one last trick.

"Well, we've kind of done all our best stuff," I said, stalling. "But maybe, if there's an outdoor space—like your driveway—we can try one more." Wright offered up his backyard instead, and we headed out through the kitchen.

The director's house was a Spanish Colonial on the east side of Los Angeles, with a deck that looked out over a pleasant green lawn bordered by bushes. Standing on the edge of the grass, I asked our host to name any playing card. He chose the five of hearts. Blake then instructed him to point to a spot of his choice in the yard. Looking out, Edgar settled on a row at about two o'clock from where we stood. As we headed over, I instructed him to dig into the mulch at the base of the bushes. Buried in the dirt, about three inches below the surface, lay a folded playing card. Edgar brushed off the dirt and unfolded the card to find—drumroll, please—the *five of hearts*!

Under normal circumstances, I'd keep the method behind a trick like this secret, but today the secret was the whole point of the story. Because Wright had asked me to illustrate the magician's process, I wanted to let him in on some of the strategies

Blake and I used. And one was that we designed each act in reverse.

Magicians start their planning process by envisioning the act's ultimate wow, the moment when something "impossible" happens—like Edgar Wright finding the exact card he'd selected in the exact spot *he* chose to dig it up. Then we work backward to identify and craft the pieces needed to bring about this effect. No amount of preparation is too much.

The three of us trooped back to Edgar's living room, where I played him a video on my iPad showing how Blake and I had loaded up.

"No way no way no way no way no way!" He shook his head with disbelief and covered his face with his hands.

Wright was watching footage of us burying fifty-two playing cards in his yard earlier that afternoon. We explained that we'd loaded up the cards in a pattern we could memorize. Then, knowing that our "magic lesson" needed to culminate in the aha moment of Edgar discovering the very same card that he'd just named at random, we reverse-engineered that discovery in order to create the illusion of spontaneity. Although Blake and I had been to the house earlier that day to bury (and video ourselves burying) the cards, when it came time for the actual meeting, we purposely showed up late, apologizing profusely, claiming we couldn't find the house. Also, we didn't offer to do one last trick; we waited for Edgar to ask us. At which point we acted reluctant and hesitant, even uncertain. We suggested doing a trick in the unadorned driveway, leaving Edgar to steer us instead to his lovely backyard. Every beat of this story had been scripted in advance.

Unfortunately, we could not reveal how we'd gotten Wright to point to the exact spot where his chosen card lay. Blake and I told him we'd debated this issue, but the technique used was a deeply guarded trade secret, and we'd be persona non grata in our industry if we gave it away.

However, the real lesson that was embedded in this story—a story he would tell and retell for years—was the lengths to which we'd gone to prepare for this trick. Our load-up was extreme, purposeful, and secret. And it yielded an impression our audience would never forget, which the story around it reinforced.

THE POWER OF NARRATIVE

"Stories are such a powerful driver of emotional value that their effect on any given object's subjective value can actually be measured objectively." This was the premise of authors Rob Walker and Joshua Glenn in 2009 when they launched a literary and anthropological experiment called Significant Objects. They began by purchasing one hundred secondhand objects at thrift shops and garage sales for an average price of $1.25 apiece. Each tchotchke was paired with an established fiction writer who created a brief story about it. Then the objects were listed on eBay, each with an accurate photograph and its invented story in lieu of a description. The listings made clear that the narratives were fictional, and the author's name was even included, so no one would mistake any story for a hoax. As anticipated, the stories raised the value of the objects. However, the *margin* of increase was a staggering 2,800 percent. In all, the power of narrative turned $128.74 worth of junk into $3,612.51 in profits, which were paid out to the authors.[1]

SPELLBOUND

THE TURK

One of the most colorful characters in the history of illusion was an inscrutable chess master known as the Turk. For eighty-four years, this mysterious sultan of strategy defeated challengers across Europe and North America, playing for, and often against, countless royals and luminaries.

Perched behind a wooden cabinet, on which he played the Royal Game, the Turk was fashioned after a Near Eastern sorcerer. He wore luxurious ermine-lined robes and sported a regal turban. A long Ottoman pipe was delicately balanced in his hand. But the most remarkable thing about him was that he was made of painted wood. What attracted audiences far and wide was the story of a mechanical man who could play chess better than any human challenger.

The Turk sprang from the imagination of Hungarian inventor Wolfgang von Kempelen in 1770. Six months before, von Kempelen had attended a wonder show in the court of Maria Theresa. The Austrian empress was so taken with the French scientist-conjurer François Pelletier's demonstrations that von Kempelen vowed to return with an even more astounding creation. Nothing like a little competition to inspire innovation.

The allure of scientific possibility also fueled the international fascination with the mechanical Turk. Before each game the inventor would open one door of the cabinet at a time to display an intricate system of gears, levers, and wheels inside the apparatus. Observers wondered, if this

⟶

WRITE THE SCRIPT

invention could play chess, what else was a machine capable of? Could clockwork and mechanics perhaps power thought?

Others decided the invention was more mystical than mechanical. And von Kempelen assisted this interpretation of the story, as well. During chess matches he would peer intently into a wooden casket adjacent to the cabinet, suggesting that its contents might be animating the Turk. Some spectators, deciding that evil spirits controlled the machine, fled before the game was over.

The legend of the mechanical marvel spread, capturing imagination and stoking fears across the Continent. In Paris, the Turk defeated Benjamin Franklin, who was serving as the ambassador to France. After von Kempelen died, a wily impresario named Johann Nepomuk Maelzel bought the Turk and pitted it against Napoleon himself. The emperor made three illegal moves, each caught by the Turk, and eventually lost by disqualification.

Finally, in 1835, Edgar Allan Poe wrote a lengthy essay about the Turk in which he hinted at its true modus operandi:

There is a man, Schlumberger, who attends him wherever he goes, but who has no ostensible occupation other than that of assisting in the packing and unpacking of the automaton. This man is about the medium size, and has a remarkable stoop in the shoulders. Whether he professes to play chess or not, we are not informed. It is quite certain, however, that he is never to be seen during the exhibition of the Chess Player, although frequently visible just before and just after the exhibition. Moreover, some years ago Maelzel visited Richmond with his automata, and exhibited them, we believe, in the house now occupied by M. Bossieux as a Dancing Academy. Schlumberger was suddenly taken ill, and during his illness there was no exhibition of the Chess Player.

Suffice it to say that William Schlumberger was a European chess master, one of several over the years who "traveled" with the Turk. As Poe himself concluded, "The inferences from all this we leave, without farther comment, to the reader."

Human beings love story. Always have, and always will, because the mechanics of storytelling and story-processing are wired into us. Back in 1944 psychologists at Smith College presented thirty-four students with a short animated film of four geometric shapes colliding and crossing at various speeds. There was no soundtrack, no text, just a circle, rectangle, and two triangles. Yet all but one of the students described the film in story terms, ascribing character traits to the different shapes and emotional motives for their movements. Most saw the two triangles as men fighting over the "innocent," "worried," and "feminine" circle. The big triangle they saw as an enraged bully.[2]

Subsequent studies of narrative instinct have produced similar results. Humans have a natural impulse to turn information *of any kind* into stories involving character, emotion, and struggle.

WRITE THE SCRIPT

Narrative instinct serves us in several vital ways. We learn through stories. We find meaning and solve problems through stories. We remember through stories. Not to put too fine a point on it, but we survive through stories.

Researchers tracing the lineage of storytelling among Aboriginal tribes have found that native stories from twenty-one disparate locations around the Australian continent describe coastal conditions that last existed more than seven thousand years ago. According to geologist Patrick Nunn, who coauthored the study, "These stories talk about a time when the sea started to come in and cover the land, and the changes this brought about to the way people lived—the changes in landscape, the ecosystem and the disruption this caused to their society." Nunn theorized that "stories endured that long partly due to the harshness of Australia's natural environment, which meant that each generation had to pass on knowledge to the next in a systematic way to ensure its survival."[3]

The best way to transfer knowledge, the early tribes found, was by combining facts—data—with social and emotional cues that engaged listeners' attention. Stories evolved as the best possible container for those elements, and all these eons later, the combination still works. In fact, according to Stanford marketing professor Jennifer Aaker, "Stories are up to twenty-two times more memorable than facts or figures alone."[4]

As social creatures, we're wired to identify patterns of human interaction. When we meet someone, our brains quickly determine whether we're dealing with a friend or foe—or a stranger who fits the *pattern* of a friend or foe. We then use those identifying patterns to help us retrieve or construct an internal story about that person's behavior, and this story shapes our responses.

SPELLBOUND

Stories also affect us from the outside in. Ever notice when watching an action movie that you get frightened or excited along with the character on-screen? As the hero fights for his life, your jaw clenches, your palms sweat, and you fidget with anxiety. This occurs because of truly magical nerve cells called mirror neurons, the brain's most essential mechanism for learning—and for story processing.

Mirror neurons fire *both* when watching or imagining a particular action, and when actually performing that action. This means, in effect, that the brains of a person hammering a nail and of the person watching him hammer the nail are mirroring each other. Or, as the saying goes, monkey see, monkey do.

These special neurons allow us to have vicarious experiences, like the surge of elation we feel when watching an athlete win a race—almost as if we'd run ourselves. Mirror neurons help babies learn not to touch the hot stove that just made their mothers scream, but to eagerly reach for the ice cream that their older siblings are gobbling with delight.[5] They allow us to merge emotionally with characters we watch on television or read about in books.

Stories also plug into our brain's social attachment system. Neuroeconomist Paul Zak has found that vicarious tension causes our brain to produce chemical messengers like ACTH and cortisol, which increase our heart rates and heighten our attention—just as it does in response to tension in real life. The more cortisol the brain releases, the sharper our focus. That's why it's so difficult to ignore someone telling a truly terrifying ghost story.

Sad, cute, or otherwise touching stories, however, cause the brain to release oxytocin, a chemical associated with care and connection. Oxytocin increases our sensitivity to social cues, especially when we see or hear about someone in need. And if the story has a happy ending, that triggers the limbic system to release the hormone dopamine, which rewards us with sensations of hope and resolution.

Thanks to this unconscious but deeply felt chemical signaling, we identify with the characters in stories and empathetically feel their pain, joy, desire, fear, and rage. We weep when reading about a dying child we've never actually met—or even seen. And we are also primed to *act* on those feelings.

In one study, Zak had his subjects watch a dramatic short film in which a father copes with his young son's terminal illness. Then he measured their oxytocin levels and compared their behavior following the film to that of a control group. He found that the film both raised oxytocin levels and made subjects much more likely to donate money to a stranger.[6]

Clearly, emotional transportation through narrative can be a powerful force for human connection, understanding, and motivation. And that makes strategic storytelling an enormously influential business tool. Or, as executive communications coach Harrison Monarth puts it, "Data can persuade people, but it doesn't inspire them to act; to do that, you need to wrap your vision in a story that fires the imagination and stirs the soul."[7]

THE ESSENCE OF STORY

Researchers at Johns Hopkins spent two years analyzing more than one hundred Super Bowl commercials to figure out if there's a particular type of story that's most successful in selling products. What they found was that the structure of the ad, *regardless of content*, predicted its success. Plot, in other words, was paramount.

SPELLBOUND

The basic plot that humans have used to tell stories for millennia has a beginning, a build to a climax, and a resolution. The plot kicks off with an incident that introduces a problem. The characters then struggle to resolve the problem, but encounter more complications. The pressure builds to a climax or showdown, when the hero of the story must make an irreversible choice. After that choice is made, the consequences fall into place, resolving the problem one way or another. In the simplest stories, such as jokes, this change takes just three acts to occur. Shakespeare more often used five acts, which gave his tales and characters a deeper sense of meaning and emotional engagement. The core structure of beginning, middle, and end, however, was basically the same.

That core structure also is used in the most highly rated commercials. This correlation is so strong, in fact, that Keith Quesenberry, the lead researcher in the Johns Hopkins study, was able to predict the most popular Super Bowl commercial of 2014. In Budweiser's heartstring-pulling spot, a puppy befriends a Clydesdale horse, only to be taken away by his human family, whereupon his buddy rallies the other Clydesdales to bring the puppy back. That commercial went viral, scoring top viewer ratings. Budweiser had hit the plot jackpot.

"People think it's all about sex or humor or animals, but what we've found is that the underbelly of a great commercial is whether it tells a story or not," Quesenberry said. "Budweiser loves to tell stories—whole movies, really, crunched into thirty seconds."[8] This is a winning strategy.

The best magic tricks, too, employ narrative plotlines. Amateurs may fall back on tired stock jokes and purchased patter, but successful magicians take care to script new stories even when performing old illusions. In the late 1980s, for instance, David Copperfield used storytelling to make a dazzlingly new version of a very old trick known as "Sawing a Lady in Half."

This illusion was originally performed as "The Divided Lady" by magician P. T. Selbit in 1921, and over the intervening decades it's become a staple of magic shows. Traditionally, the magician presides over the sawing procedure. But Copperfield's "Death Saw" turned the magician into a superhero in a Houdini-esque escape scenario structured in three cinematic acts.

Act one: A giant spinning blade looms above Copperfield as he struggles to free himself from his constraints before the timer hits zero. And Copperfield fails! Time runs out, and the blade plunges into Copperfield's midsection, cleaving the magician in two.

Act two: a surreal sequence in which Copperfield interacts with his cloven body. Over dreamlike music, his lower half is spun around to face his torso. "Move your feet!" an audience member shouts from the back of the house. And Copperfield moves his feet to prove that no artificial limbs are involved. But how will our hero become a whole man again? This will be the climax of the story.

Act three: Copperfield gestures to the clock and rewinds its hands. In dramatic slow motion, as time is reversed, the two halves are rejoined, the saw blade goes back up. Copperfield stands, restored.

The audience cheers as much for the emotional journey they've taken with their hero as for the illusion itself. The story has exposed them to danger, fear, hope, humor, surprise, as well as the sweetness of victory and relief. It's this story, the *narrative container* for the technical feat, that leaves them feeling invigorated as they exit the theater. And it's the story that they'll remember to tell their friends.

SPELLBOUND

HEROES IN ACTION

Throughout his long entrepreneurial career, Ted Turner has garnered a reputation for being a wild, impetuous risk-taker. His business deals, like his approach to yacht sailing, are often described as brash, unpredictable, flouting convention. As one *New York Times* reporter put it after Turner successfully defended the America's Cup in 1977, this captain of industry and the sea brought to mind "a variety of heroes from Mark Twain and Horatio Alger to Errol Flynn. What adjectives fit? Take your pick. Flamboyant, volatile, charming, witty, handsome, outrageous, disrespectful, uncouth, irreverent, jaunty, courteous, rude."[9]

Turner's character fits neatly into the myth that Americans love to tell about the brave and rugged entrepreneurs who built this country. In corporate America, especially, daredevils are admired and well compensated for their courage. Generous stock options are frequently defended as incentives for CEOs to take risks. In this mythology, the heroic entrepreneur is, by definition, one who'll put everything on the line in order to succeed.

When Malcolm Gladwell trained his analytic eye on the heroic story of Ted Turner, however, he found that the real Turner is not what he seems.[10] As a businessman, Gladwell wrote in a 2010 examination of entrepreneurship for the *New Yorker*, Turner calculates the odds of every transaction, regarding the marketplace purely as a source of opportunities that everybody else undervalues. "Turner is a cold-blooded bargainer who could find a million dollars in someone's back pocket that the person didn't know he had. Once you get past the more flamboyant aspects of Turner's personal and sporting life, in fact, there is little evidence that he had any real appetite for risk at all." Still, the swashbuckling image sticks.

⟶   **WRITE THE SCRIPT**

Most of us are culturally steeped in the mythology of the daring hero, almost from the time we're born. Stories from the Bible to *Star Wars*, from *Little House on the Prairie* to *The Lord of the Rings*, have trained us to equate heroism with the *illusion* of risk. And this indoctrination isn't limited to Western culture. The Bhagavad Gita, the Koran, and folklore all over the world pit brave heroes against heavily armed villains. When it comes to attracting attention, a heroic story will trump careful analytics, every time. No surprise, then, that industry titans and magicians alike paint themselves as heroes.

Illusionists often appear onstage to be taking incredible risks as they exercise their mysterious "superpowers," and in general, they work hard to seem as uniquely memorable as fictional characters. However, illusionists who present themselves as infallible often find their audiences rooting against them. Daredevil magician Criss Angel has achieved phenomenal success in part because his spectators secretly hope he'll fall into the alligator pit. But this persona leaves him no room for error.

I've chosen to create a different kind of hero for my act. Playing more of an underdog, I never invoke supernatural elements. The impossibilities that I conjure are direct results of science and practice, and I make no bones about that. Unlike most magicians, I tend to wear failure on my sleeve—which belongs not to a black velvet costume but to an ordinary "layman's" shirt or jacket. My character is one of imperfect genius—an absent-minded puzzle-maker engaged in such complicated intellectual juggling that from time to time he misses a calculation. Instead of announcing himself as a hero up front, he lets his deeds speak for him—even when his deeds are less than impressive.

SPELLBOUND

I've discovered over the course of countless performances that this flawed character affords me the breathing room to make mistakes, such as dropping a card on the floor, or incorrectly guessing a word. I'd prefer an errorless show, to be sure, but the hiccups tend to humanize me, making it easier for the audience to identify and sympathize with me. Even more strategically, after I've made a few mistakes, the audience will doubt my ability to nail the finale of my show, in which all the pieces from previous tricks come together in a giant puzzle. This heightens the drama and turns the trick into a true climax by raising the stakes. I have to surpass myself in this one last test if I'm to earn my heroic stripes as a Comeback Kid. Of course, I always do, but the audience's uncertainty makes my ultimate victory that much more rewarding for us all.

It's all part of the scripted story.

When it comes to corporate marketing, the underdog brand of hero can be just as valuable as the Captain Courageous illusion. Slogans that highlight humble beginnings and triumph over adversity are used by small and large companies alike. Nearly thirty years on, Ben & Jerry's continues to remind consumers that its founders opened their first ice-cream store at a lowly gas station, with amateurish hand-drawn logos. Nantucket Nectars' label tells us that the company started "with only a blender and a dream," and Apple's garage roots are an integral part of the company's history and brand.

Which type of characterization will be most appealing depends on the audience. Professor Anat Keinan and her colleagues at Harvard Business School conducted a number of experiments to test a hypothesis that consumers who identified with being an underdog would respond more to underdog brands than to top-dog brands.

Indeed, Keinan found that "the stronger a subject's own 'underdog disposition'—a sense of struggling in tough circumstances—was, the greater his or her preference for the underdog brand."[11]

Like the myth of the risk-taking entrepreneur, the underdog hero seems to be embedded in the American psyche. So both types of hero can star in potent narratives. Just make sure to know your audience before you decide which one to cast.

STORIED STRATEGY

In the spring of 2008, as Barack Obama's bid for the Democratic presidential nomination was picking up speed, a story hit ABC News that Obama aide David Axelrod later described as "a missile directed right at the heart of our campaign." After announcing on national television that Rev. Jeremiah Wright, Obama's pastor and mentor for twenty years, had a penchant for "inflammatory rhetoric," reporter Brian Ross played a video of Wright preaching "God damn America" for its unequal treatment of black citizens.

"God Bless America?" Wright demanded. "No, no, no, not God bless America. God damn America—that's in the Bible—for killing innocent people. God damn America for treating us citizens as less than human. God damn America."

Although Wright had married the Obamas and baptized their two daughters, candidate Obama had already taken steps to distance himself from the fiery preacher after an article appeared about him in *Rolling Stone* one year earlier. In fact, that article had prompted Obama to rescind an invitation for Wright to give the invocation at the official launch of his campaign. "We can't afford to let this story hijack the day," Obama had said at the time.

SPELLBOUND

But Wright's quotes in the *Rolling Stone* article—that "racism is how this country was founded and how this country is still run," and that Americans believe in "white supremacy and black inferiority and believe it more than we believe in God"—paled in comparison to the damning orations being broadcast and rebroadcast across the country in March 2008. This archived footage, which blindsided the campaign, posed an existential threat to Barack Obama's candidacy.

The campaign desperately needed to change the story, and only the candidate himself knew how. He told Axelrod, "I want to do a speech on Wright and the whole issue of race in America. We have to try and put this in a larger context or it's just going to go on and on."

Five days after ABC began running the Wright footage, Barack Obama stepped up to the podium at the Constitution Center in Philadelphia and told a story that he'd scripted almost entirely himself. This acutely strategic story began with the words "We the people." It told of the "improbable experiment in democracy" that had produced a constitution that was "eventually signed but ultimately unfinished" because of "this nation's original sin of slavery" and its legacy for successive generations of Americans.

In this context, Obama then told his own story:

I am the son of a black man from Kenya and a white woman from Kansas. I was raised with the help of a white grandfather who survived a Depression to serve in Patton's Army during World War II and a white grandmother who worked on a bomber assembly line at Fort Leavenworth while he was overseas. I've gone to some of the best schools in America and lived in one of the world's poorest nations. I am married to a black American who carries within her the blood of slaves and slaveowners—an inheritance we pass on to our two precious daughters. . . . I will never forget that in no other country on Earth is my story even possible. It's a story that hasn't made me the most conventional of candidates. But it is a story that has seared into my genetic makeup the idea that this nation is more than the sum of its parts—that out of many, we are truly one.

Obama then turned directly to the issue of Jeremiah Wright's language, condemning it as divisive and offensive. He called Wright's view "profoundly distorted" but also told a different story of Wright as the minister, public servant, and former marine who helped introduce Obama to his Christian faith. He could no more disown Wright, he said, than he could disown his white grandmother, "who on more than one occasion has uttered racial or ethnic stereotypes that made me cringe."

He went on to describe the conditions that stoked prejudice among both black and white Americans, aspects of race and racism that needed to be addressed openly and honestly by all sides, to achieve "a more perfect union."

The way Barack Obama took hold of the Wright story and strategically reengineered it astonished even seasoned political pundits, many of whom initially had thought the campaign was finished. "By taking on the explosive issue of race so directly and personally, Barack had transformed his own political crisis into an occasion for national reflection," Axelrod later wrote in his memoir, *Believer: My Forty Years in Politics*. "The world, and even those of us closest to him, got new insight into how he would deal with the crushing pressures and complex challenges of the presidency. Our opponents had hoped the Wright tapes would tear him down . . . instead he never looked more presidential."

Strategic stories like the one encapsulated in Obama's speech are designed to serve a purpose. They can be used to inspire, to motivate, to change opinions and behavior. They are often told to highlight the values of the organization or brand. But underlying the purpose usually is a problem that gives the story a dramatic sense of urgency.

In a sense, Obama had been telling his story of race and responsibility for years, playing the low-key hero as a community organizer even before entering politics. But when the Wright crisis introduced the vital plot element of overt racial divisiveness, that original story ignited. Instead of ducking it, Obama embraced divisiveness as the dramatic problem the story needed to solve—by making America itself the hero who ultimately triumphs against racial discord and distrust.

The challenge was to direct this story in a way that was both consistent with Obama's own values and also likely to restore his campaign's threatened image. The candidate's willingness to come right out and confront the issue of race in America turned out to be the strategic plot twist that surprised and amazed, creating the illusion that the campaign had been prepared for such a crisis all along.

Not all strategic stories deal so directly with the problem they're intended to solve. Instead they may revolve around a proxy challenge, as did the tale that legendary magician Jean Eugène Robert-Houdin used to assist Napoleon III in North Africa in 1865.

————————→   **WRITE THE SCRIPT**

At the time, Algerian spiritual leaders, called Marabouts, were exhorting their followers to rebel against the French colonial government. Napoleon coaxed Robert-Houdin out of retirement to help him quell the unrest by undermining the Muslim prophets' influence. The idea was to use illusion to tell a story of the superior power of the Christian West. Or, as Robert-Houdin wrote in his autobiography, "to prove to the Arabs that the tricks of their Marabouts were child's play, and owing to their simplicity could not be done by an envoy from Heaven, which also led us very naturally to show them that we are their superiors in everything, and, as for sorcerers, there are none like the French."[12] In other words: France's imperialist magic is the strongest in the land.

For weeks Robert-Houdin toured the disputed territory, performing in theaters and at special gatherings of tribal chiefs. In the climactic act of each show, he held aloft a small wooden box and asked for the strongest, most powerful man in the audience to join him onstage. Robert-Houdin then announced that he had the magical power to strip this muscular hero of his strength. To the audience, of course, this seemed an impossible task. Indeed, on his first try, the volunteer would lift the box with ease.

But then, with a wave of his hand, the magician exclaimed, "Now you are weak." When the tribesman next attempted to lift the box, it wouldn't budge. He'd strain and strain, but appear to have lost his power.

As Robert-Houdin later wrote, one frustrated man tried to rip the box apart, but when he touched the handle, he reeled backward, howling in pain and terror, and ran out of the theater. Audiences were both wowed and cowed back into submission. The demonstration convinced them that no Marabout could possibly compete with the superpowers of the French.

SPELLBOUND

Now, it might seem as if Robert-Houdin deceived his audience. In fact, his superpowers had nothing to do with mysticism. The master magician, who was fascinated by science and technology, had simply concealed an electromagnet beneath the stage to make the box immovable. He also ran an electric current through the handle to shock recalcitrant volunteers. But all the illusion was really intended to demonstrate was power, and in that respect it involved no deception at all. After the fact, Robert-Houdin instructed his Arab translators to explain to the chieftains, "My pretended miracles were only the result of skill, inspired and guided by an art called prestidigitation, in no way connected with sorcery."[13] Science prevailed over superstition, and three days later thirty of the most powerful local leaders presented Robert-Houdin with an illuminated manuscript praising his art. They also pledged their allegiance to France.

The line between illusion and deception can be so fine that sometimes it's simply the emphasis of the story that tips the balance. The Mast Brothers learned this the hard way after they'd been trading on their passionate origin story for nearly a decade.

According to this tale, Mast Brothers chocolate company, the hipster pride of Brooklyn, was founded by two bearded brothers who in 2006 began grinding cacao beans from Guatemala and Ecuador and churning them into chocolate in their Williamsburg, Brooklyn, apartment. The story highlighted the brothers' heroic commitment to locally sourced ingredients and exacting control. It presented them as uniquely authentic characters who produced a uniquely authentic product, and it appealed to chocaholic foodies who gobbled up the narrative of "do-it-yourself chocolate bootstrapping."[14] The success of this narrative depended either on its being true, or on the complicity of all who actually knew the brothers when they launched their business.

$\longrightarrow$ **WRITE THE SCRIPT**

For years the Mast Brothers' strategic story served them well. They opened three shops, won the favor of uberchef Thomas Keller, and sold an array of elegantly packaged chocolate bars to high-end retailers across the country. Then rumors began to circulate that, in fact, the brothers had initially "remelted" mass-produced industrial chocolate instead of making their first bars from scratch, as they claimed. Early photographs turned up, revealing that—horrors!— they hadn't even had beards back then.

Finally, in late 2015, food blogger Scott Craig compared the Masts to the lip-synching singers Milli Vanilli, and wrote that they'd been serving up an illusion wrapped in a story from the start. The brothers were forced to admit that they had initially used industrial chocolate. Even though they insisted this had been just a passing phase before they developed the bean-to-bar process that's now central to their brand, the damage was done.

Remember, the chocolate that their customers had adored just weeks earlier still *tasted* exactly the same. All that had changed was the public's perception of their story. Yet in the weeks after Craig's exposé was posted, sales of Mast Brothers chocolate at some shops plunged as much as 66 percent over the preceding year.[15] Critics continued to accuse the brothers of deceit. All because they'd anchored their story in an illusion of artisanal authenticity that they could not support.

Protect your wow factor. Illusion usually bends the truth, but the story it tells should never hinge on an outright lie.

WHAT'S *YOUR* STORY?

The stuff of story is all around us. While the particular form your narrative takes will depend on the problem you need to solve, there really are no limits to the material you have to choose from. Even data can be turned into story, as the online dating site OkCupid makes clear in its blog, OkTrends, one of whose posts opened:

Picture this online dating scenario:

1. You see someone you like.
2. You read their profile, and wow.
3. You send them a long message.
4. You hang tight and . . .
5. . . . you never get a reply.

Sadly, this is a typical story. Even on a lively site like OkCupid, only about a third (32%) of first messages get any response.

But, the story continued, OkCupid was coming to the rescue of those ignored lonely hearts! Playing the hero of this story, the dating site offered hope in the form of data that revealed the optimal length of messages ("shorter is better") and the optimal order of contact ("over 40% of female-to-male first messages *do get replied to*"). In later blogs, the data were even more helpful, offering insights such as the best question to ask if you want to know whether someone will be willing to have sex on the first date. (Answer for both men and women: "Do you like the taste of beer?" It seems that nearly 70 percent of women and nearly 90 percent of men who like beer will consider first-date sex. . . . Go figure.)[16]

Jawbone, maker of fitness trackers, also has a blog, which posts both customer stories about using these monitors and feature stories constructed out of raw data collected from the devices. One data story on the blog traced the sleep of people living near the

South Napa earthquake in Northern California in 2014. Reading that 93 percent of Jawbone UP wearers bolted upright at 3:20 a.m., you can't help but feel a vicarious jolt yourself, imagining the strength of the shaking and fear that kept 45 percent of those closest to the epicenter up the rest of the night.[17] This post paid itself forward through hundreds of mentions in the mainstream media and other blog sites—all terrific free advertising for the company.

The king of data storytelling online is Nate Silver, whose FiveThirtyEight blog has been heroically aggregating poll numbers since 2008. In 2012, the site correctly predicted the top vote-getters of the presidential election in all fifty states. But the success of the site depends not just on getting the data right but also in crunching the data into stories such as "Why FiveThirtyEight Gave Trump A Better Chance Than Almost Anyone Else," an article by Silver three days after the 2016 election, using data to show that Silver was still king—even after his predictions this year proved wrong. In every case, it's the meaning of the data that story ultimately delivers.

Heritage is another strong source of material, not only for advertising and marketing purposes, but also for stories that help solve management problems. In the late 1990s, executives at UPS realized that their operations were outmoded and they needed to revamp the entire way their company did business. Being efficient at moving packages was no longer enough; UPS needed to develop new services. This meant changing the way employees understood their jobs. The company's history couldn't change, but the *story* that executives told about that heritage now took on a new emphasis. In this narrative the company had always been a heroic innovator, daring to shift from bicycle deliveries to trucking, to building the world's second-largest cargo airline, and then introducing online package tracking. UPS employees were more than service engineers. In fact, the story showed, they'd always been innovators who embraced and prospered through change. And so they had nothing to fear as the company now began its new and necessary experiments to keep pace with the future.[18]

Heritage also served the narrative purposes of Kraft Foods after it acquired the British confectioner Cadbury in 2010. There had been stiff opposition to the merger from Cadbury's management and forty-five thousand employees, and the business press, smelling disaster, was telling the story that the two company cultures were incompatible. Kraft needed to come up with an alternative story, and fast. Since the fear at Cadbury had to do with the loss of their firm's traditional values and product quality, Kraft dug into its own archives for evidence that such fear was unfounded. The result was an intranet site called "Coming Together," which told the similar stories of the two company founders, James L. Kraft and John Cadbury, both men of faith who prized and defended quality, fairness, and community. The site included a visual road map of Kraft's history of mergers, showing how Kraft maintained the integrity of acquired companies while making them stronger. The story told on the site was repeated by executives through press releases and employee training sessions, and revolution was averted.[19]

But if the past can provide story fodder, so can engagement in the present, especially when the story makes the *audience* an active participant. All magicians know this well. It's why almost every magic act involves audience volunteers. More and more companies are learning the same lesson.

In 2010, Molly Fienning was peering up into the bright afternoon sky in Beaufort, South Carolina, watching her husband, Ted, land his Marine Corps fighter jet. She was sporting Air Force–issued aviator sunglasses, the same given to every pilot and their wives. But suddenly Molly looked at the other families around her on the flight line and noticed that the kids were all squinting and rubbing their eyes—staring straight into the sun without protection. And the idea for Babiators was born.

But how to get parents to spend twenty dollars on quality UVA-protected sunglasses for kids, when children are notorious for breaking or losing their glasses? The Fiennings consulted their partner Matthew Guard's business professor, who suggested that they couple Babiators with an "irrational offer": a lost-and-found guarantee. The company would promise customers an absolutely free pair of replacement sunglasses if their originals were broken or lost within one year of purchase.

The plan was counterintuitive. Wouldn't unscrupulous consumers take advantage of the offer and scam the company for a free pair of glasses? Molly told Bloomberg TV, she hoped so. "You do have those people who seek out their free pair, but those are the most enthusiastic brand ambassadors. So yes, you gave a free pair, but then you might have sold four or five more because of that one free pair."[20]

The notion of partnership is paramount to Babiators' branding. "Our Story" on the company's website introduces customers to two couples who met in college. Their mission is "to protect kids' eyes while they're out exploring this awesome world." And they back up this mission with an extraordinary customer service policy because they believe in "kids being kids." With this story and a kitchen table as an office, the Fiennings and the Guards launched a business that quickly grew to become one of *Forbes* magazine's 100 Most Promising Companies in 2014. Today Babiators has sold a million pairs of glasses, with projected sales north of $7 million in 2017.[21]

Themes of benevolence and concern for humanity and the planet run through many brand stories today. The toothbrush company Smile Squared, for example, donates one toothbrush to a child in the developing world for every brush a customer buys, thus making the customer an active participant in the story of global engagement that began when company founder Eric Cope visited Guatemala and learned how many children contracted preventable diseases because their families had to share toothbrushes. Strategic story consultant Ty Montague calls companies that employ these kinds of engagement narratives "storydoing" companies.

One thing that differentiates story*doing* from story*telling* companies is that the story of doing starts with senior leadership and affects every department, every employee in the organization. The story isn't simply a marketing narrative used in ads; it drives policy and gives meaning and a larger purpose to the commercial aspects of the business. And it invites clients and customers both to play significant roles in the narrative, and to share and spread the story through their own social networks.

Montague's consultancy, co:collective, has found that storydoing companies have several major advantages over storytelling companies. After comparing the data from forty-two publicly traded companies in categories ranging from retail and entertainment to online services and transportation, Montague reported that storydoing companies generate *twenty times* more mentions in social media than do their storytelling counterparts, and those mentions are more positive. Companies that employ an engagement narrative also spend far less on paid media and have a faster growth rate.[22] The lesson here is not just that people love feel-good stories, but also that audiences love to feel that they're *part* of those stories. So much so that they'll reward companies that give them this feeling by paying their stories forward.

⟶   WRITE THE SCRIPT

INDIAN ROPE TRICK

Perhaps the most mystical trick of all is one that has blossomed solely in the imagination of the spectator. The Indian rope trick was just such a phantasm.

On August 9, 1890, the front page of the second section of the *Chicago Tribune* featured an article about two Yale graduates, Frederick S. Ellmore and George Lessing, who'd witnessed an extraordinary miracle by a street fakir in India. The article recounts that the wonder-worker tossed a ball of twine into the air but "instead of coming back to him it kept on going up and up until out of sight and there remained only the long swaying end." Then a boy appeared and like a "monkey climbing a grape vine" scaled the rope until he vanished at about thirty to forty feet. Ellmore quickly snapped photos and Lessing sketched the scene.

But the developed photographs didn't match the sketches. In fact, the film showed nothing of the sort: no boy, no rope, just the fakir sitting on a ragged carpet. Ellmore emphatically concluded, "Mr. Fakir had simply hypnotized the entire crowd, but couldn't hypnotize the camera."[23]

The story spread like wildfire. It was the perfect amalgamation of mystical elements at the right time in history. Hypnotism was a popular yet little-understood practice and the newly colonized India was the land of mystery. Readers wanted to believe, and this script, penned by one John Elbert Wilkie, gave them all the evidence they needed.

After months of inquiries, however, the *Tribune* printed a retraction. The story was a hoax. Wilkie apologized: "I am led to believe that the little story attracted more attention than I dreamed it could, and that many accepted it as perfectly true. I am sorry that anyone should have been deluded."[24] Fred S. Ellmore, it seems, was concocted to "sell more" newspapers.

But the truth was revealed too late. The frenzy in the public imagination persisted as firsthand accounts of the Indian rope trick now poured into circulation. Historians began to find parallels to the rope trick in ancient stories from Marco Polo and the fourteenth-century traveler Ibn Battuta. Even today some claim to have witnessed the trick.

As for the legend's fabulist, John Elbert Wilkie went on to become the director of the U.S. Secret Service from 1898 to 1911.

COMMAND THE TAKEAWAY

The most important part of any strategic story is its takeaway—the final impression it makes on the audience. That impression is, inescapably, an illusion.

If you listened to the popular first season of the podcast *Serial* in 2014, you know that one of the most vexing aspects of its investigation into the true-life murder of young Hae Min Lee of Baltimore was the unreliability of witness testimonies. Even those who testified immediately after Hae's death gave contradictory versions of what they thought they'd seen, heard, and been doing themselves

WRITE THE SCRIPT

at the time. One expert in false witness statements told host Sarah Koenig that this was absolutely predictable, since "people tend to bend their memories to what they think the police want to hear." Without even realizing what they're doing, in other words, *eyewitnesses* serve up illusions, which then masquerade as truth. In criminal investigations these dubious takeaways can have life-or-death consequences.

If you don't happen to wear a detective's badge, the best way to command someone's memory is to control the tail end of their experience. Researchers at the University of Toronto did this—quite literally—by tweaking the final moments of a standard colonoscopy for one of two groups of patients.[25] Both groups were given the normal procedure, in which a scope is inserted into the gastro-intestinal system, and as the camera made its internal inspection both groups reported the same amount of discomfort during the actual procedure. Only with the second group, the doctor left the instrument in place for about twenty extra seconds, without moving it. The test lasted a little longer for them, but, unlike the first group, their final sensations were painless. That takeaway of ease was all it took to reshape their memory. When the patients later were asked to describe their experience, the second group remembered the procedure in much rosier terms than did the first group. And this recollection directly affected their behavior even years later, when the second group turned out to be much more likely than the first to return for their next routine colonoscopy.

Magicians know full well that memory is an illusion *and* that illusion can command memory. This is why the false recap holds a cherished place in every magician's narrative toolbox.

The false recap is the performer's summary of the events the spectators have just witnessed. The description will sound accurate, but in fact it's been tweaked strategically to control the impression that audiences will take away.

In magic this tweaking can be designed to deceive. For example, let's say I've shuffled the cards and had a man in the front row cut them. Later in the act, I might say, "Let's review: Sir, you shuffled and cut the cards." Most audience members will accept this enhanced version of the story because they remember the man handling the cards. Often, even *he* won't remember that it was actually I who shuffled.

The false recap can also play out on a much grander scale. I'm now going to let you in on a secret that I've been waiting years to reveal. Remember my performance at Edgar Wright's house—climaxing with the buried cards? Well, that performance was scripted specifically to lead up to a false recap.

As you'll recall, our visit that day ended with our showing Wright the video of Blake Vogt and me burying cards. However, *there were no buried cards*. Blake and I had indeed gone to the house earlier in the day to shoot the video, but we only made it *appear* as if we'd buried all those cards. (Remember, cinema, like magic, takes advantage of the gap in viewer perceptions.) When the moment came to impress Wright by "unearthing" his five of hearts, we actually used sleight of hand.

Our script was designed to impress Wright with the idea that magicians will go to insane extremes to load up their illusions. Preparation was the point of the story that we wanted him to remember, so our false recap left him with an impression of insane preparation that he'd never forget. We were certain that, long after we'd left his house that day, Wright would wander out into his yard and poke around in the dirt, searching for the rest of those fifty-two cards. We knew he'd go on wondering, trying to puzzle out what had really happened. He'd tell his friends that the real secret of illusion is to make absolutely sure you're many steps ahead of your audience. And *that* part of our false recap would be absolutely true.

Deception aside, the false recap can serve a valuable purpose in business simply by shifting the point of emphasis that you want your audience to remember. Let's say you've just given a presentation that covered a boatload of information, some of which you were required to deliver, some of which you're not entirely sure you even agree with. A technically true recap would remind your audience of all the main ideas you've just covered, but that won't leave them with the impression that you *want* them to take away. Fortunately, it's your job as presenter to sum up the most important points for them. So you tweak your recap for emphasis, perhaps add a little personal editorializing, and leave them with the impression that matters most for them to remember.

The false recap can also be used strategically to spin the credit. As health care employment specialist and former magician Janet Elkin explained to the *New York Times'* Adam Bryant, "A former boss of mine would remind me: 'Don't take the credit. It's easy to take the credit, but you don't have to. Give it to somebody else. It will come back to you.' Even when things were your idea, nobody has to know that." So you spin a false recap, congratulating your associates for a job well done. That way they buy in, "and then you give them a chance to feel that they can take the next step."[26]

The best-told stories, like magic acts, are always the ones that the audience pays forward.

4

CONTROL THE FRAME

W hen Franklin Delano Roosevelt decided to return to politics after being stricken with polio at age thirty-nine, he faced a serious image problem. The norm at that time was to keep the disabled out of the public's sight and mind. A physical handicap was a source of shame that many associated with mental or moral flaws. It was also emasculating, since manly men in Roosevelt's era were expected to be physically fit and visibly strong. Masculinity was an absolute requirement for higher public office in the 1920s, so this posed a special obstacle for FDR, who was paralyzed from the waist down. After spending seven years unsuccessfully trying to rehabilitate his legs, he knew that actual recovery was impossible. If he wanted to succeed, he had no choice but to resort to illusion.

He'd been setting the stage for this act almost from the beginning of his illness. He'd orchestrated his public appearances so the press never witnessed him being carried or wheeled, or manhandled into or out of a car or train. He also cultivated an indomitable, heroic demeanor that exuded absolute confidence and strength of character, with the help of symbolic props. He'd wave his signature cigarette holder to signal cheer and optimism. His pince-nez spectacles reminded people of the popular two-term Democratic president Woodrow Wilson. And FDR was always smiling, affable, joking as if he'd never heard of pain or failure. When he appeared at the 1924 Democratic National Convention in Madison Square Garden to support New York governor Al Smith's run for president, however, FDR faced a special challenge. This was his first major public appearance since his paralysis, and he felt that his own political future depended on his ability to "prove" that he was recovering. He would not be seen in a wheelchair.

Roosevelt had his son James case the convention hall in advance to scope out the widest and least obstructed entrances and aisles. Each day FDR arrived well before the other delegates, to be loaded into a special oak chair placed near the front, with arms solid enough to keep his body stable. He spent all day in that chair, except when he gave his speech. Then he had to "walk" to the speaker's platform. In part, this performance was a feat of endurance. He supported the dead weight of his legs by lifting his upper body onto a crutch on one side while gripping James's arm on the other. Iron braces kept his hips and legs from buckling, but these were camouflaged, the braces painted the same black as his shoes and socks. Meanwhile, aides discreetly followed, just far enough away to be out of the spotlight, but close enough to spring to the rescue if Roosevelt toppled. The intensity of FDR's grip nearly made his son cry out in pain as they inched their way to the waiting area.

Roosevelt wouldn't allow anyone to help him the final fifteen feet to the podium. He hoisted himself onto two crutches and laboriously dragged his legs forward. By the time he finally reached the lectern he was drenched in sweat.

Suddenly, FDR tossed back his head and flashed a grin that encompassed the entire arena. This display of monumental effort bought him cheers of sympathy and admiration. But Roosevelt's true mastery of illusion really shone once he began to speak, because he made the audience essentially forget what they'd just witnessed. As biographer Hugh Gregory Gallagher wrote in the aptly titled *FDR's Splendid Deception*, "From the first he had the complete attention of every person in the hall. He spoke in his fine, clear tenor, and he spoke with powerful effect . . . the audience, already moved by his courage, was soon swept up by the power of his delivery."[1] FDR's finish that day was met first with awestruck silence, then an explosion of applause that lasted an hour and fifteen minutes—setting a record for Madison Square Garden.

Four years later Roosevelt returned to the convention, this time envisioning his own trail to the presidency. Now it wasn't enough to appear to be recovering; he had to make the public believe he'd actually triumphed over his handicap and was fully capable of holding higher office. He couldn't use crutches this time, because crutches were the symbol of pitiful cripples, like Dickens's Tiny Tim. The last thing a presidential contender wanted to arouse was pity. So FDR and his son Elliott this time devised an illusion to make audiences think he really could walk:

> Elliott would stand, holding his right arm flexed at a ninety-degree angle, his forearm rigid as a parallel bar. Roosevelt would stand beside Elliott, tightly gripping his son's arm. In his right hand Roosevelt held a cane. His right arm was straight and held rigid with his index finger pressed firmly straight down along the line of the cane. In this posture, he could "walk," although in a curious toddling manner, hitching up first one leg with the aid of the muscles along the side

of his trunk, then placing his weight upon that leg, then using the muscles along this other side, and hitching the other leg forward—first one side and then the other, and so on and so on. He was able to do this because his arms served him in precisely the same manner as crutches. His right arm transmitted the weight of his body through the index finger along the full length of the cane to the floor. His left arm, leaning on his son's arm, similarly took the weight off his body.[2]

FDR's team had made sure in advance that the lectern was bolted and solid enough to hold his weight, so once he safely reached it he could hold himself upright with his hands and arms. This may sound easy, but remember that he was holding the weight of his entire body in his arms. To convince the audience that he was at ease, he used his head to gesture and his smile and voice to convey complete command. His performance was carefully designed to distract the audience's focus *away* from the physical reality that FDR wanted them to ignore, while directing their attention *toward* the image and rhetoric he wanted them to respect and remember when it came time to vote for him, first for governor of New York, and then, again and again, for president of the United States.

Franklin Delano Roosevelt demonstrated in these appearances, as he would many times over in his political career, that he was a master of the skill that illusionists call misdirection.

THE MAGIC OF MISDIRECTION

In magic, misdirection refers to the controlled diversion of audience attention away from the *method*, or mechanics, of the illusion and toward the illusion's sensational *effect*. Some modern magicians use the arguably more accurate term "attention management," but either way, this is the means by which we make audiences think that we have the power to vanish and transform objects and otherwise defy the laws of physics—to make the ordinary seem extraordinary. Smoke and mirrors sometimes come in handy, but the essential skills here require no special props. In fact, four-year-old children use the most basic form of misdirection every time they point across the room to steer competitors away from their hidden cache of cookies. Capuchin monkeys do much the same when they raise false alarms of danger to stop competitors from finding their bananas. Athletes use a more sophisticated form when they fake a play in basketball or feint a dummy pass in soccer or rugby.

The type of misdirection used in illusion, however, requires a conscious command of the gap between what audiences notice and what they don't. A magician's goal is to amplify that gap so the audience never even suspects the real work behind the effect. As FDR proved, this skill can serve anyone who wants to control the way an image, message, product, or policy is received.

One key to misdirection is a focal tool that magicians call the "frame." This is the specific area where they want the audience to look, witness, and enjoy the culmination of the trick. It's generally *not* where the mechanics of the trick are happening, since those take place in the shadows, the gray zones the audience never notices. Am I holding up this cup because I've materialized a lemon inside? No, I'm creating a frame to hold your attention while I use my other hand *outside* the frame to steal an orange from below the table.

Sometimes the audience can see the area outside the frame, but they don't realize it's relevant. One of magicians' favorite methods is the "bold move," a tactic that is brazen and risky, particularly fun to pull off. These bold moves usually involve placing an object outside the frame but still within view—if you know where to look. For example, let's say I'm performing a three-coin routine:

1. I reach out and pluck the first coin out of the air, and set it on the table.
2. I reach up to materialize number two, and place it on the table beside the first.
3. I extend my arm a third time for the last coin . . . but come up empty.
4. "Where is the third?" I ask the audience. "Why, it's *already on the table*." And sure enough, there is the third coin, sitting next to the first two, as if by magic.

The technique is simple, though it can only be accomplished by a magician who's skilled at moving the frame: While my left hand reaches for the third coin, moving the frame up and away, my right hand, naturally dangling at table level, stealthily places the third coin.

In one of his most famous routines, the great sleight-of-hand artist Tony Slydini used frame control to fool only the volunteer onstage, while letting the rest of the audience in on the trick. It hinged on the volunteer looking downward on the paper balls that the magician was rolling between his hands. When Slydini flicked his arm up, he tossed the ball over the volunteer's head, just out of his field of vision. This action was *in* frame for the audience but just out of frame for the participant, who was fooled every time. The audience, marveling at the volunteer's unwitting blindness, howled as a stack of paper balls accumulated on the floor behind him.

SPELLBOUND

If you think of the frame in terms of a camera's viewfinder, you can see how the practice of illusion has changed for magicians who perform on television. Famously, Penn & Teller exploited the TV frame during a trick dubbed "Are We Live?" for *Saturday Night Live* in 1986. While making cards, a lightbulb, electric drill, and doll all appear to levitate, Penn repeatedly asked the studio audience, "Are we live?" Their cheers confirmed that the audience at home was seeing a live, unedited performance. What the home audience could not see, however, was the frame in which the magicians were operating—and within which the camera was positioned. Both Penn & Teller and the camera were hanging upside down, suspended with their feet secured to the studio ceiling and a crossbeam positioned to look like a table at their waist. The apparent defiance of gravity was actually just gravity doing the trick for them!

The whole point of "Are We Live?" was to demonstrate how powerful the frame can be in controlling audience perspective. Misdirection determines not only what people see, but also, and even more critically, what they comprehend.

This idea became the basis for an episode of the radio series *This American Life* after the show's producers learned of a woman named Mary Archbold, who had been "hiding in plain sight" for most of her life. More specifically, what she'd been hiding was the fact that she had only one arm.

Archbold had been missing that arm since birth, so she operated as an adult in ways that, to her, seemed perfectly natural. It was only to avoid social awkwardness that she directed *other* people's attention away from her prosthesis. What made this more difficult was that Archbold is an actor, a dancer, a performer, and a Pilates teacher. She's always onstage. And yet, most of her dance partners never noticed that she had only one arm. Her students didn't notice. Her audiences didn't notice. Not even the boys she dated in high school had noticed!

Archbold's techniques include always wearing long sleeves and, like a magician, using big gestures, big expressions, and moving quickly so people don't have time to see that her wrist and fingers don't move.

"I stand on a certain side so that they really only see my real arm," she told host Ira Glass. And she's always careful to keep her working hand ready for action. "Like at a party, I will not hold a drink in my hand. I will take a sip and set it back down, because if I meet somebody, they're going to want to shake my hand." If she needs to demonstrate a movement in her Pilates class, she simply calls on a student to be her model.

But what about those boys she dated back in school? Most of the time, the same techniques of misdirection worked with them, too. Even if the shirt came off, the left sleeve would always stay on. "If there was a shirt open," she asked rhetorically, "are you going to be looking [for my arm]?"

Archbold's techniques, Glass marveled, are "so simple that hearing them makes you realize how easily tricked we all are, how unobservant we are in so many situations." This is precisely what makes misdirection possible![3]

ON-BEATS AND OFF-BEATS

The concept of the spatial frame works in tandem with timing units that we call "on-beats" and "off-beats." On-beats are like temporal frames, in that they're the *moments* when a magician signals the audience to pay attention. During the on-beats, spectators tense up and concentrate because they think the trick is happening before their eyes. The off-beats are the other moments, when the audience relaxes their focus because they think nothing important is happening.

- On-beat: I present a coin in my left hand, close my fist around it, and stare at it intently. This has the effect of shrinking and tightening the frame.
- Off-beat: I glance up, crack a joke, relax my shoulders, maybe brush the debris from the last trick off the table. Suddenly the frame widens but also loses focus.

This frame shift occurs because the audience responds to the off-beat as a natural or inadvertent break in the action, a chance to relax. As the renowned Dutch magician Tommy Wonder explained, "When an audience relaxes, their attention broadens, spreading out over a wider and less carefully observed field." In other words, they see more, but notice less. My casual posture and joke prompt my audience to laugh, and because it's difficult for anyone to focus when they're laughing, this off-beat is precisely the right moment for me to ditch the coin.

After finishing my joke I then resume the on-beat and direct everyone to look back at my left fist. Whereupon, with a flourish, I'll fan my hand open to show that the coin has "vanished," and people gasp.

This reveal offers me another off-beat that I can use to set up the next trick. That's because awe is also a powerful distractor. The most difficult time to think critically is when you're surprised, applauding or turning to your neighbor to ask, "Did you see that?!" So if a magician "finishes" his routine by producing a large parrot flapping its colorful wings, you can be sure he's using this moment to load up for his next move, perhaps stealing another parrot while taking a bow.

There's a branch of magic called "manipulation," which arguably is the most difficult kind of stage magic to perform. It's sleight of hand in full view—pulling cards, coins, Chinese fans, birds, etc. out of thin air. No saw-a-lady-in-half boxes, no crates, or panels. One person, center stage. What makes manipulation so difficult is that the frame is largely fixed—all eyes on the magician at all times. His control of on-beats and off-beats is paramount. Right there, in front of everyone, he is tuning the audience's attention up and down, as if manipulating a virtual knob.

- On-beat: He reaches up with his right hand and plucks a fan of cards out of the air.
- Off-beat: He smiles and takes applause (while stealing more cards).
- On-beat: He makes the stolen cards appear suddenly in his left hand.
- Off-beat: With both hands occupied, he casually drops the cards into a hat (while stealing flowers, say, from the hat).
- On-beat immediately followed by off-beat: He walks to the front of the stage (far from the hat) and makes a huge bouquet of flowers appear. And while the audience takes in this impossible grand finale, he's secretly setting up his next trick.

Clearly, all this involves intensive preparation, a strong command of the act's narrative thread, and a practiced ability to multitask—to perform more than one action and think more than one thought at the same time. These are vital skills in the art of illusion, as they are in life. But they don't require supernatural powers. What they do require, at least in order to gel as misdirection, is a keen understanding of the ways that human attention both functions and falters.

ATTENTION, PLEASE

Let's start with a basic reality: Your brain is a liar. How could it not be? The truth is that we are each surrounded by gazillions of stimuli, from subatomic particles to galaxies far, far away, not to mention yapping dogs and chatty children, beams of sunlight, blinking cursors, demanding bosses, lists of errands, aching feet, potential customers, yellow roses, vibrating cell phones, expectant audiences, and, of course, Facebook, Twitter, YouTube, Instagram, Snapchat, and the entire social media universe . . . All Competing For Our Attention Every Waking Second Of The Day.

If we had to attend to each and every stimulus all the time, our brains would fry within nanoseconds. A task like that requires a supercomputer that would dwarf anything currently even imagined by human beings. Just to handle all the *visual* information around us, according to one neuroscientist, "Our brain would need to be bigger than a building, and still then it wouldn't be enough."[4] Fortunately, evolution has presented us with a fairly effective workaround: our minds only process a fraction of reality.

We may think we observe the world around us "accurately," but in fact our perceptions are constantly being filtered and adjusted by a host of cognitive processes involving multiple neurological circuits. What we register as reality is an illusion—a minuscule fraction of the information that's actually there. That's because our brain has evolved to present us either with the information that our subconscious decides we need to survive, or that we deliberately pluck from the myriad possibilities. Then our neural circuits edit out the extraneous details that would otherwise overload our cerebrum.

Attention is as central to this process as a camera operator is to the making of a film. Attention determines which perceptions will be brought into focus *and* which are given priority. Or, as William James wrote way back in 1890 in his *Principles of Psychology,* "It is the taking possession by the mind, in clear and vivid form, of one out of what seem several simultaneous possible objects or trains of thought."

Those objects and ideas don't just seem to be simultaneous, though; the immediate competition for the mind's attention is most definitely limitless. Which means that even the most perceptive and observant individuals will miss information directly in front of their eyes. Magicians count on this.

And yet, attention is a marvel of flexibility. Just like a camera operator with a zoom lens, it can tighten focus to the very limit of sensation. A grain of sand? A twinge in your side? The fragment of a seed stuck between your teeth? No problem. In fact, the smaller and more discrete the target, the easier it is for most of us to focus on. And when our focus is relatively narrow, it's easier for us to sustain our attention, even while performing other, more automatic activities, such as walking.

Widen the spotlight of attention, however, and you'll find you have more difficulty keeping your concentration steady. Picture a packed theater with all the house lights on as the stage fills with costumed actors busily pushing props, shaking hands, and pretending to talk to each other. Meanwhile a cell phone rings in the audience, and the red exit light starts to blink, and the usher below you seats a woman wearing a huge white plumed hat. Where do you look? What do you notice? How can you tell what's important? Chances are, within your widened spotlight, you'll either choose to zero in on one point of interest, or else you'll pick up on a couple of prominent images that share certain qualities. For instance, you might simultaneously be able to track the two women onstage wearing bright red and black dresses. But the rest of the scene will then recede out of focus.

Now imagine the house lights going dark and the stage lights dimming as a spotlight singles out one actor stage right who starts to sing. Where does your attention go? What happens to the scope of your focus? If you're like most human beings, your gaze and your attention will fly directly to the center of this actual spotlight.

A similar process occurs every time you step into a new "scene" in daily life, though without the assistance of stage lights. For instance, it would be impossible to take in all the details of your company's annual meeting the instant you enter the boardroom, so your brain naturally does a quick scan, then shrinks its spotlight to a more comfortable scale. That scale allows you to focus on the CEO at your mental spotlight's center, while people and objects on the fringes fade from notice, and everything outside the light's margin goes blank. Then your attention will selectively move its spotlight here and there, sharp on the clock in the corner one minute, then to the tapping of the chairman's pen on the podium, then to the person now speaking, while the other faces around the table and the print of the document under discussion grow blurry.

This spotlight effect (a term psychologists attribute to James) extends to all kinds of mental focus. If you've ever tried to talk to someone who's completely engrossed in a book, you know that attention can both blind and deafen us to our immediate surroundings. We attend to whatever holds the center of our focus, and become more or less unconscious to the surround sound.

The kind of highly selective concentration that it takes to read that book is what neuroscientists call "top-down" attention, because it's cued by conscious thoughts in the brain. The harder we consciously try to pay attention, the more neurons fire in the cortex of the brain, which is responding to that stimulation, but at the same time, neurons in the surrounding regions are actively being *suppressed*. It's as if the brain has coded all competing information as irrelevant and shut the door on it. This suppression intensifies the spotlight effect and dulls or cancels out involuntary, or "bottom-up," attention, which reacts to unexpected sights, sounds, smells, and other signals from the body's sensory system.

Now, some bottom-up stimuli may get through, no matter what. Someone taps you on the shoulder, and even if you're engrossed in a book or text, you'll probably look up, all attention turning to the source of that tap. The more sensational and insistent the demand—a shot, a scream, a flash of light—the more likely it is to interrupt voluntary attention. But subtler or more remote signals don't have a chance. This is why magicians try to make their off-beat moves quiet and unobtrusive—so as not to disturb the audience's voluntary attention.

At the same time, they work hard to *heighten* that top-down focus. "Watch me like a hawk," an illusionist will command, knowing full well that, as *Now You See Me*'s catchphrase put it, "the closer you look, the less you'll see." That's because, the more you strain to see something, the more you'll miss around the edges of your spotlight, where the secret moves are actually happening.

All this explains why more than half of all traffic accidents involve cell phones. Despite what we might wish to believe, the mechanics of attention make human beings notoriously poor multitaskers. When desires or distractions make it impossible to choose between stimuli, our attention might alternate, but the spotlight does not easily split. Drivers who text or talk on the phone—even a hands-free phone—tend to devote their top-down attention to their conversations, making road cues compete for focus. As a result, these drivers are slower to detect problems on the road, slower to react to obstacles, and have less control over their vehicle's speed, lane positioning, and headway.[5] Some studies have found they're even more attention-impaired than drunk drivers.[6] The bottom line? A child running into the road thirty feet ahead won't stand a chance unless your concentration as a driver is *both* undivided and also relaxed enough to let your involuntary, bottom-up attention kick in.

One way to achieve that level of relaxation is through mastery of the focal activity. Magicians know this. That's why we practice maneuvers many thousands of times over periods of years, until the moves actually become reflexive. Famed illusionist Teller likes to tell a story about practicing the cups and balls trick in a midwestern diner one day when one of the balls rolled out of his control, momentarily distracting him. Without his even realizing it, his free hand continued loading another ball under a cup. Likewise, some trained Morse code operators are said to be able to carry on a conversation while decoding whole messages. I, too, find I'm able to shuffle and control playing cards while talking about an entirely different topic.

CONTROL THE FRAME

Scientists call this "overlearning." The skill is so thoroughly mastered that it becomes an almost autonomous function, thus freeing up some of the neurons that performance would normally require. Sorry, all you cocky teenagers, but this means that being a *new* driver only adds to your likelihood of having an accident while texting.

Another type of attention that magicians use shamelessly is "joint attention," a communal form of focus triggered by eye movements and body language. Joint attention comes so naturally to humans that, if adults in the room are paying attention to one individual, any babies present will also turn to that person.[7] This reflex has evolved to help facilitate communication, like an invisible social organizer. In social interactions, the signals that control joint attention are so subtle that it's difficult to describe this process as either voluntary or involuntary. Have you ever had the sensation that you were being watched in your car, only to glance in the rearview mirror and meet the direct gaze of the driver behind you? The conscious and subconscious always work together, but this cooperation is especially evident in joint attention. All a magician has to do is shift his gaze to the left, and *as if by magic*, the whole audience will move the frame of their attention to see what he's looking at.

Kind Snacks CEO and former magician Daniel Lubetzky finds this particularly useful as a leader. "Where you look is where people look. I think it's a very good tool among many that you learn as a magician. How to guide human emotions and dynamics."[8] In this sense, gaze is like a shortcut to the mind.

Gaze can also be a window *into* the mind. Researchers have shown that we tend to look longer at choices we prefer, a finding that prompted Pizza Hut to introduce the first "subconscious menu" in the United Kingdom in 2014. Customers merely look at pictures of menu options on a tablet, and the eye-tracking software orders for them. But the tablet also offers a button for them to change the order if its prediction was wrong. Pizza Hut is trying to assist, not *direct* customer decisions.

A study published in 2015, on the other hand, proved that eye movements can be used to manipulate people. Participants were asked serious moral questions, such as, "Is murder defensible?" Then they were shown the words *yes* and *no*, side by side. The researchers found that 58 percent of participants chose whatever response they were looking at when asked for an immediate answer. By timing the demand for an answer to a certain eye direction, the interviewer could influence the responses. According to one of this study's authors, "The processes that lead to a moral decision are reflected in our gaze. However, what our eyes rest on when a decision is taken also affects our choice."[9] Putting a cheery spin on findings that some might find chilling, the director of the Eye Think Lab at University College London pointed out that today's mobile phones can easily be equipped with sensors to track eye movements. "By documenting small changes in our behavior, our mobiles could help us reach a decision in a way that has not been possible before." Of course, mentalists have been doing this for ages.

In one classic mind-reading trick, the "telepath" wagers that he can guess which of your hands contains the coin. Try as you might to conceal the secret, the mentalist is aware of your "tells"—which hand is squeezed tighter or the imperceptible tilt of your head in the direction of the coin. Likewise, when you're selecting from a spread of playing cards, you can bet the magician is tracking your gaze— even if it *seems* like he's engrossed in the joke he's telling you.

$\longrightarrow$ CONTROL THE FRAME

What we notice is one aspect of attention, but what we think it means is quite another. We have to decode the limited information our brains do collect before we can decide what to do with it. So behind our inner camera operator sits a cognitive director who's constantly interpreting the significance of whatever our mental spotlight illuminates. Confuse that inner director and you wind up with cognitive illusions—magicians' stock in trade.

It's not difficult to create this confusion, since the brain generally assigns just one meaning at a time to every image it notices. Cognitive illusions occur when you assign the *wrong* meaning to something you've observed. Let's say you watch me hold out a rope. Because of the way I'm holding it, your brain decides that it's just one continuous rope, can't possibly be two. So when I snap my fingers and produce two ropes, you think I've done something "magical." That simple trick would never work if you could hold two opposing interpretations of an image at the same time.

As a magician, I count on your brain to tell you that I can't simultaneously put something into a bowl and take something out of it. You'll assume I'm bending down to tie my shoelace because my shoelace has come undone. One action, one purpose. I scratch my neck because it itches. I move the pen across the page because I'm writing. The single assumed purpose dominates your attention so that you don't even notice me slipping a card under my shoe, or dropping a coin down my collar, or pushing a pen up my sleeve as I'm writing. Magicians say they're "informing the motion" when they hide a secret move inside an action that seems to serve an entirely different purpose. FDR was using a slightly more transparent version of this tactic when he "leaned" on his son Elliott in order to "walk."

The classic optical illusion called Rubin's vase provides a good illustration of our inability to process multiple meanings simultaneously.

One moment, you look at the drawing and see two faces looking at each other. Look again, and you'll see the vase. If you try to see both meanings in the drawing at once, your visual processing system will resist, creating a flickering sensation as your brain switches the interpretation of the image back and forth.

The Stroop effect, named for the American psychologist who studied it in the 1930s, also shows how hard it is for our brains to handle competing simultaneous meanings. J. Ridley Stroop found that when subjects were asked to read the names of colors written in ink of a different color, such as the word *red* printed in blue, they

Rubin's Vase

took much longer and made more mistakes than they did when reading the words in black or in colors that matched the word.

The same principle applies to actions. When people speak, for example, they often gesture with their hands, and their listeners assume that the purpose of the gestures is to reflect or emphasize what's being said. A 2010 study found that listeners are actually stumped if the gestures *don't* match the words—for instance, if the speaker twists an invisible rag while saying "chop." As with the Stroop effect, when asked to describe what they were hearing, volunteers watching the incongruous gestures were slower and less accurate in their responses—even if instructed to concentrate *only* on what was being spoken.[10]

This is worth remembering if you have to speak in public or make presentations as part of your job. Make sure to look at the screen when you project a new slide, and use your body language to direct audience attention toward the information you want them to absorb. Otherwise, their attention will be torn between the visual stimuli and the words you're speaking. What's worse, your words may not get through at all. That's because hearing and vision share a limited neural resource, and unless the signals are working together congruently, the audience is more likely to focus on the visuals than on what they're hearing. If your words and gestures both speak to the images, however, there's no competition, so your message will come through loud and clear.

MULTIPLE METHODS

Juan Tamariz of Spain, revered as one of the greatest living magicians, coined the term the "theory of false solutions" to describe the process of a magician systematically eliminating all possible solutions until the only remaining explanation is *real magic*. Simply put, if a stage illusionist makes his assistant disappear from a paneled box on a rolling table, he might remove each panel, one by one, to demonstrate that she is not hiding behind any of them—to eliminate those "solutions." When the last panel is gone, the audience might conclude that she's hiding behind the rolling table. Then, because he baited the audience into suspecting this, the magician will rotate the table with great flare to show that she's not concealed there, either. Having never entertained the solution that the illusionist's assistant sneaked offstage, or hid beneath the table, the audience at this point is convinced, she must have *vanished!*

Another technique the magician often employs is a second illusion that contradicts the assumed explanation for the first one. The dancing handkerchief routine, which cleverly utilizes unseen strings, often culminates with the conjurer placing the suspended silk within a corked clear jug. Somehow, the silk continues to dance *inside the jug*. How could the magician puppeteer the handkerchief if its container is completely sealed? The cleverly designed jug is the second illusion that "disproves" the audience's initial assumptions. It misdirects the audience away from the belief that strings are involved in the first part of the trick.

Last, an adept conjurer will vary methods throughout the arc of a trick. For example, if he is causing a card to rise to the top of the deck again and again, each time he will vary the sleights used. Maybe the first time he uses palming, the second time false shuffling, and the third time a duplicate card. By using wildly different executions each time, but presenting a singular effect, the magician prevents the audience from latching on to any single explanation.

Cognition not only has difficulty processing contradiction, but it's also slow to react to change. When an image is flashed onto a screen but changed slightly with each repetition, most people don't notice the alterations. And when volunteers were asked to watch a video of a burglary in one 2010 study, 62 percent failed to notice that the identity of the burglar changed halfway through the crime.[11] Scientists call this "change blindness."

The brain is slow in many ways to register changes in sensory information. For instance, we all continue to see images and feel sensations for a brief period after the source is gone. If I place a coin in the palm of my hand, you'll still see the shimmer of it after I secretly sneak it away. It's as if an impression of a gleaming circle has been burned into your retina.

Thieves, as well as magicians, take advantage of cognitive afterimages. Theatrical pickpocket Apollo Robbins, for example, can steal the watch right off your wrist, and you won't even know it's gone until he returns it. That's because Robbins will first find an excuse to grab your wrist, which sends a perception of the watchband through your neural circuits. Moments later, when he slips the band into his pocket, you'll have the illusion that you're still wearing it.

SPELLBOUND

another cognitive factor in attention is our sense of purpose. Let's say you're trying to find the building where you're going for a job interview. Chances are, your girlfriend could be waving at you just a few feet away, and you wouldn't notice her. Researchers call this "inattentional blindness," and it's one reason why bystanders who are present at the scene of a crime are not necessarily useful eyewitnesses. In general, people notice only what their subconscious tells them they need to notice in any given situation—and everything else is pushed out of frame. The stronger the sense of purpose, the less extraneous sights and sounds register.

One of the best-known demonstrations of inattentional blindness was orchestrated in 1999 by the University of Illinois's Daniel Simons: "We showed people a video and asked them to count how many times three basketball players wearing white shirts passed a ball. After about thirty seconds, a woman in a gorilla suit sauntered into the scene, faced the camera, thumped her chest and walked away. Half the viewers missed her. In fact, some people looked right at the gorilla and did not see it."[12]

Inattentional blindness explains why frames play such powerful roles in misdirection. The harder you try to figure out what's going on during an on-beat or inside the frame of my actions, the more latitude I have to maneuver outside the frame or during an off-beat. What I'm actually doing is taking advantage of your cognitive limits.

DIRECTION AND DISTRACTION: THE ESSENCE OF MISDIRECTION

Misdirection plays as central a role in business as it does in magic. Whether you're competing for a job, launching a new product, promoting a brand, or just conducting a meeting, you need to successfully direct your audience's attention toward your message while distracting them away from information that would diminish its impact. But while magicians try, as much as possible, to direct and distract simultaneously, these two phases don't necessarily have to overlap to be useful in your life.

Active direction of your audience's attention engages and reroutes their conscious thoughts. In effect, you're creating an onbeat and instructing them to focus their mind on your frame. Central to this process is what Tommy Wonder calls "the concept of offering something of greater interest."

One way to actively interest an audience is to pose a new question—or an old question in a new way. A question is like a mental frame for focusing an issue, and many people default to familiar questions the way kids default to their favorite toy. So, as every clever politician knows, one of the most effective ways to misdirect interest is to challenge audiences with a different question than the one they've been using to frame their opinions.

There is arguably no better way to shift attention away from unwanted news than by posing a suggestive question about the person who delivered that news. In the 2016 presidential primaries, this tactic was on display every week, if not daily, as Bernie Sanders responded to primary losses by raising questions about Hillary Clinton's "judgment," and Ted Cruz parried attacks from Donald Trump by raising questions about Trump's ties to a mafia-linked felon. Meanwhile Trump deflected debate questions he didn't like by posing questions about moderator Megyn Kelly's fairness. Each new question moved the spotlight of attention in a direction that served the candidate's interests—at least until the next question was thrown into the ring.

SPELLBOUND

A little-known initiative at Royal Dutch Shell has been using questions in a very different way, posing them as scenarios, to actively direct attention of company executives toward meaningful solutions. Long Term Studies was launched back in 1965 at Shell's London headquarters when then–program director Ted Newland and his team noticed that most people in the organization were planning for the future by extrapolating from the present. People do tend to cling to the familiar, especially to ideas that work for them in existing circumstances. How, then, to actively redirect their focus to future events and conditions that could radically change these circumstances and render their ideas useless? Newland found that scenarios offered the most effective way to capture executives' attention and change the questions that shaped their thinking. In his words, "You are trying to manipulate people into being open-minded."

By coming up with future scenarios such as tightened government restrictions due to a global energy gap, or sharply rising inflation and wages due to war in the Middle East, or a tilt in geopolitics to favor Asian markets, the team prompted divisions throughout the company to turn their attention to the ways that all would have to work together, from risk managers and strategic planners to public affairs operators and engineers, to react in the event of such changes. In Newland's opinion, "The greatest value of scenarios is that they created a culture where you could ask anyone a question, and the answer would need to be contextual. Answering, 'Because I'm the boss' or 'Because the business case is positive' was out-of-bounds."

Or, as his colleague Pierre Wack put it, "Strategic vision is not driven top-down by a corporate leader but involves the capacity to ask the right questions and to be amazed."

$\longrightarrow$ CONTROL THE FRAME

Executives around the globe seem to agree. Not only has Shell been using scenario planning for more than forty-five years, but 65 percent of large (over $2 billion in revenue) companies surveyed by Bain & Company in 2011 also used this tool to direct executive attention.[13]

It's often said in magic that "a big move covers a small one," as when an illusionist makes a broad sweep of his arm to obscure what his hand is doing. This works because the eye is automatically drawn to the dominant motion and cannot simultaneously attend to minute movements within it.

But not all covering moves are literally big. The introduction of motion on a still stage, high contrast against a dull background, a loud sound, or conflict in an otherwise peaceful setting will all reliably attract attention, not because the audience consciously chooses to shift focus but because they can't help it. Their senses make them do it. When a magician uses this technique to distract audiences, it's called passive misdirection.

One of the most effective ways for an illusionist to passively misdirect spectators is to introduce something new into the frame. Let's say I'm going to lift up a cup to reveal a ball. It's more effective to "kick" that ball so that it rolls across the table. Virtually every eye in the audience will track the path of that ball. Likewise, I might use "flash paper" to create an incendiary burst, automatically diverting your eyes.

The appeal of novelty is almost irresistible because it's hardwired into us. In evolutionary terms, this made humans more likely to explore and discover new sources of food, mates, and survival strategies. In marketing terms, this makes us susceptible to novel packaging, ad campaigns, and flavors. Bianca Wittmann, whose research at University College London showed that the reward centers of the brain light up with activity when we're exposed to new choices, explains, "I might have my own favourite choice of chocolate bar, but if I see a different bar repackaged, advertising its 'new, improved flavour,' my search for novel experiences may encourage me to move away from my usual choice."[14]

Of course, familiarity also has a certain comforting appeal, and brand loyalty is the holy grail of most corporations. So the idea is not to introduce an option so wildly different that it alienates or confuses established customers. Coca-Cola learned this lesson the hard way after introducing New Coke in the 1980s. Loyal Coke drinkers felt that the basic formula of the soft drink was too sacred to mess with, and their backlash forced the company eventually to discontinue the product. The company still uses novelty to direct attention to the brand by introducing new packaging and flavors such as Cherry Coke, Coca-Cola Black Cherry, and Coca-Cola with Lime, which build on the original formula, but the illusion here is that the consumer can buy something new without giving up the old. This way, Coca-Cola benefits from both impulses.

Confusion is another guaranteed way to distract people. Or, as Sun Tzu wrote in *The Art of War*, "The whole secret lies in confusing the enemy, so that he cannot fathom our real intent." But the target needn't be an enemy, and the goal needn't be to defeat. By injecting a subtle contradiction or distraction into an ordinary conversation, you can interrupt the other person's focus, and that will give you the power to redirect the conversation.

This strategy, which social psychologists call the "disrupt-then-reframe" technique, is a potent tool for sales and persuasion, as University of Arkansas researchers discovered in 1999, when they went door-to-door selling boxes of Christmas cards for a local charity. The sales and charity were legit, but three different sales approaches were tested. All began with a standard pitch for the center for the disabled that would benefit from sales of the cards. But at one third of the stops, the customer was told, "They're 300 pennies. . . . That's $3. It's a bargain." Another set of customers was told, "They're $3." And the third group was told, "They're $3. It's a bargain." In this experiment, and in three more variations that followed, disrupting the charity sales pitch by saying, "They're 300 pennies," and then reframing the charitable contribution as "a bargain," more than doubled sales over the other approaches.[15]

This technique has long been used by hypnotists. One of the first to write about its use in a clinical setting was Milton H. Erickson, who found that most people who came to him for treatment were also somewhat leery of hypnotism. The tension between their desire for help and their resistance to the mode of therapy created a barrier that needed to be broken before he could help them. So Erickson deliberately confused them at the beginning of the session. He'd drop a non sequitur into a sentence, or offer an unexpected handshake, or garble his speech slightly. This disruption made people more likely to comply with whatever he suggested next.

Both Erickson and the Arkansas researchers found that the successful formula was consistent. A suggestion had to be made, then disrupted, and reframed quickly. Reframing *before* or *without* the disruption didn't work nearly as well. It also helped if the audience was predisposed to cooperate. The holiday card customers, like Erickson's patients, had good reasons to agree, from the outset. Most wanted to help the local charity and could use the cards, but there were also plenty of reasons to resist someone turning up at the door to sell them something they hadn't asked for. Disrupting-then-reframing got them over that small bump of resistance. However, subsequent experiments have found that it's not as effective in hard-sell situations.

Another important aspect of this technique is its subtlety. As magicians know, the most effective distractions are low-key and seem to occur within the natural flow of events. Just as a loud bang onstage will yank audiences *too* far out of the spell of the act, disruptions that have nothing to do with the initial conversation could confuse customers so much that they'd grow frustrated, suspicious, or annoyed. The goal is always to manage attention, never to threaten it.

WATCH *THIS*: OVERT MISDIRECTION

We live in a world of physical misdirection. The meat and poultry most of us eat, for example, is raised and slaughtered far, far away from customers—sometimes under conditions that would give them serious pause, if they saw them—then packaged and displayed in such a way that kids in America can grow up without having any idea that meat comes from animals. The illusion is that grocery stores produce food.

In the same way, most people who drive a car have no idea how it runs. That's because automakers take great pains to design pleasing exteriors that misdirect attention away from the mechanics as effectively as a magic wand. In the case of the sleek, classic Jaguar XJ series, so many customers were enchanted into buying the cars, only later to discover that their $50,000–100,000 had bought them breakdowns, leaks, and parts failures, that a secondary market grew up around "Jaguar conversions." Mechanics who knew how to look past the visual frame—and under the hood—would swap out the Jaguar engine with a more reliable and powerful one in order to sustain the illusion that Jaguars can drive like a Corvette.

These are examples of "overt misdirection," a term coined by neuroscientists Stephen Macknik and Susana Martinez-Conde to describe techniques that steer an audience's visual and/or spatial frame away from the messy truth of the underlying process by shifting the physical presentation of the effect. Every company that produces a "user-friendly" product is engaging in this type of attention management.

The catch is that, like a great magic trick, these products often depend on internal workings that are brilliantly complex—and which their engineers would doubtless love to show off. It takes a leader like Steve Jobs, who can appreciate *both* the technical wizardry and the need to present customers with a simplified and appealing interface, to maximize the misdirect. The genius of Apple products is that they appear to be simple enough for children to use, and indeed, children *can* use them, but there's nothing remotely simple about the work that produces this illusion.

Swedish behemoth IKEA also uses overt misdirection to prevent customers from seeing what's really behind their promise to deliver well-designed furniture at "breathtaking prices."[16] Consumers may think their own willingness to assemble IKEA tables and chests at home is what makes them economical, but they have no idea how complicated the systems are that make "some assembly" possible. Production behind the scenes is broken up into teams that are devoted to finding new ways to make each step in the chain more efficient. One team focuses exclusively on maximizing the number of plates that a pallet can hold. Another found that by increasing the density of particleboard at stress points in furniture, they could reduce it elsewhere, thereby lowering costs while making furniture more durable. This is how IKEA has been able to drop the price of the BILLY bookcase by 76 percent since its introduction. But as far as the public is concerned, it might as well have happened by magic.

Overt misdirection in business isn't limited to manufacturing. It can also play a role in professional management and service delivery. It may even be *necessary* in professions like medicine, which emphasize transparency. If the combination of misdirection and transparency sounds like an oxymoron, consider the dilemma of doctors in a liver transplant ward where patients and family members are now included in discussions during teaching rounds. Rounds conversations used to be restricted to the medical team involved in each patient's care, but new policies of transparency have opened them up. Traditional Socratic teaching practices, however, have not changed. Residents are still questioned about each patient's condition and asked to make diagnostic and treatment recommendations. What if these new doctors blunder in front of the family members? More than a loss of face could be involved; the doctor and hospital both could lose credibility. Residents might be reluctant to venture an opinion, thus compromising both their own education and the patients' care. What's more, if the case is particularly difficult, the patient and family's anxiety could be intensified by witnessing the debates and problem-solving that necessarily go into a complex diagnosis and treatment protocol. The solution? Misdirection.

In the liver transplant ward at the Cincinnati Children's Hospital Medical Center, surgeons and residents meet prior to rounds to discuss each case. This way, diagnostic and treatment conferences and teaching can occur outside the "frame" of patients and their families. Then, when they conduct rounds, the medical team can reveal the effects of their deliberations without showing the messy process behind them. As one doctor explained, "We actually do the pre-rounds to get everyone on the same page." It helps the team "come up with a solidified message so that when we talk in rounds in front of the family, the plan is clear."[17]

VIRTUAL MAGIC: COVERT MISDIRECTION

While "overt misdirection" creates an illusion by changing the audience's physical frame, "covert misdirection" achieves the same goal purely by messing with their mental frame. Magicians use off-beats and cognitive illusions such as change blindness and inattentional blindness to misdirect covertly, but in business subtler psychological trickery comes into play.

Salespeople use covert misdirection all the time. Consider the tactics that Realtors use to give an empty house the illusion of home. They'll "dress" it with just a few neutral but tasteful furnishings from a rental company (perhaps one that does nothing *but* dress houses for sale, since this has become an industry unto itself). They'll bake cookies just before the open house so the whole place smells like Mom's waiting for the kids to come home. And they'll strategically place framed photographs of babies and small children, but none of adults. Why? Because many home buyers need a nudge to envision their own, perhaps future, family in this setting, but at the same time, buyers are a little like dogs who want to find and mark their own tree, and they'll pass if they see evidence that the competition has marked it first.

SPELLBOUND

This kind of covert strategy can even misdirect appetites. Researchers have found that when people use small plates, they serve themselves—and eat—30 percent less than when they use a plate twice as large. These results have been confirmed in studies all over the world, regardless of the type of food served.

What's fascinating, though, is that the reframing doesn't work if people know they're being observed. That is, if they know their eating is the object of someone else's attention, the plate loses its power to misdirect their own attention, and they wind up eating *more*.[18]

To master covert misdirection, then, you need to be able to crawl virtually into your audience's mind, view the situation from their perspective, and figure out how to frame the idea you want them to accept. This is exactly what credit card companies did in the 1970s, when some retail merchants started imposing a surcharge on credit purchases to cover the 1 percent that credit card companies charge retailers. Consumers saw that the cash price was cheaper, and hesitated to use their cards. An attempt to equalize the pricing by law failed in Congress, so the credit card companies were forced to use misdirection. They simply persuaded retailers to reframe the credit card price as the "regular" price, and offer a reduced cash price as a "discount." Suddenly, instead of feeling scammed, consumers felt that the very same two-tiered pricing offered them a bargain.

The warehouse giant Costco engaged in a similar reframing maneuver when it positioned its chain as an exclusive club, rather than as a box store. Cofounder Robert Price decided that customers would need to have an American Express card to join. As he told NPR in 2015, he envisioned "a speakeasy where somebody would feel, gee, I've got this special deal. And I can come in and shop, and most people can't come in and get in here." He even instituted bouncers (aka security guards) to keep you out if you're not a Costco member. And for the privilege of shopping there, you pay $55. Which incentivizes you to shop at the heavily discounted chain (and not elsewhere) in order to recoup your membership fee in savings.[19]

But Price didn't stop there. He also wanted to misdirect customer attention away from the tedium of shopping and toward the fun of hunting for bargains. So he turned his gargantuan warehouse stores into unmarked mazes of discount treasures. "I was adamant that we would not have signs telling people where things were, because that would make it likely that they would wander through all the aisles and find other things to buy." And so it does. Consumers zigzag through the store, constantly discovering unexpected temptations. This wouldn't be possible if they entered the store with the mindset they usually bring to the grocery store. It works because they perceive Costco as an entirely different enterprise. That's an illusion, of course. They still come home with a car full of groceries (give or take the occasional big-screen TV), but the misdirection pays off handsomely for Costco, whose annual sales top Amazon's.

SLEIGHT OF TIME

Just as our eyes play tricks on us when confronted with optical illusions, so our minds frequently construct time illusions. Our perception of time, like taffy, is subject to stretching, shrinking, and reversal. This time shifting can be manipulated for effect. Let's call this "sleight of time."

SPELLBOUND

Casino managers are keenly aware of the relationship between time and attention. That's why gambling floors never feature clocks or windows to the outside world. Left to their own devices, committed gamblers will pour all their energy into the game they're playing, and, as with any voluntary attention, this will blind and deafen them to other stimuli. It will also stretch their sense of time and mentally distance them from other demands *on* their time, be they flight schedules, or jobs, or family duties. The presence of a wall clock or daylight could threaten this illusion of infinite time, so casinos don't take that chance. They covertly engineer sleight of time.

Strictly speaking, the term "time misdirection" in magic refers to the use of time to distance method from effect. Much as casinos want to prevent gamblers from suspecting that their rolls of the dice are keeping them up past dawn, magicians want you to lose track of the actions that set up the trick. Let's say you leave your phone on the table as you head into another room for a moment. I might pop off your phone's case, fold up a playing card, and put the case back on over it—the perfect setup for an impossible revelation. But the pitfall would be to perform the trick the second you return. You'd immediately associate your absence with my opportunity for mischief. And so I wait. If I do the trick an hour or two later, especially if it's someone else's idea to see a card trick, the discovery of the card will seem much more magical.

Temporal distancing can serve a valuable purpose in business, too, as Nick Chasinov learned when he was building his online marketing firm Teknicks. Having initially tried to launch the start-up with*out* a time delay, after one year he was forced to get a day job. Wisely, he went to work first at a digital marketing firm and later at Lexis-Nexis and McGraw-Hill. What he learned through these jobs was that his original Web design business model for Teknicks was flawed, because it banked on one-time customers. What he needed to offer was search engine optimization (SEO) and Internet services to clients on an ongoing or recurring basis.

Throughout his employment, Chasinov continued to quietly load up in preparation for Teknicks's relaunch. He met many future clients. He noticed the services that were most in demand. He scouted talent among the freelancers who worked for his employers. Though careful not to poach his colleagues or steal business from his bosses, he was stealthily building a strong financial and knowledge base for his own firm. After five years, Chasinov was ready to quit his day job.

Having hidden the messy start-up of his young venture behind a screen of time, Chasinov was able to spring the polished result on the public as if by magic. In 2009, he not only signed his former bosses as clients, but he also made $1 million in sales. By 2011, he had thirty-four employees and sales of $2.5 million.[20]

"Spontaneity" that's planned like this not only makes for an impressive introduction, but also reduces the risk of competition. What your opponents don't know, they can't copy. So if you have an ingenious idea that you want to present to your CEO, your best bet is probably to develop it stealthily on your own time, at night and over weekends, until you're sure you've worked out the kinks and made it bulletproof. Then, when the magic moment arrives, you can be sure it will make you look like the *only* genius who could pluck this kind of brilliance out of thin air.

But what about *reversing* time? I've said throughout this book that a key goal in magic is to always stay at least "one step ahead" of the audience. Typically, this means glimpsing a card or otherwise knowing a key piece of information in advance, or loading an object into position without being seen. But sometimes it means reversing the natural order of events, to get chronologically ahead of *ourselves.*

I used this strategy in 2010 to bring about what would eventually become my big break. The *New York Times* had heard about the crossword puzzle–magic fusion that I'd debuted two months earlier at the Magic Castle, and their science writer Cornelia Dean wanted to interview me for an article about it. That was pretty exciting, of course, but I figured that a video piece on the *Times* website could make an even bigger splash. So I suggested to Dean that, because the crossword trick is very difficult to describe verbally, it might be helpful if she see it in person. Better yet, perhaps she'd like to shoot a video of it for the *Times.* I was planning to perform at a private party in two weeks, and I'd be happy to add her to the guest list. Except, I had no party scheduled.

What I *did* know was that it wouldn't be difficult to set one up. So I banked on finding a suitable living room where I could do a show. And, as soon as she accepted the invitation, I went to work. Fortunately, when you tell people that the *New York Times* wants a nice home in which to record a video, volunteers do indeed line up.

We filmed the piece, and two weeks later it appeared, much to my surprise, on the front page of the *New York Times* online. In addition, the *Science Times* featured an article about my process for creating crosswords that push the envelope. The article announced that I was pioneering a new type of magic, one that appealed to the intelligentsia. Because my parents are both academics who'd harbored more than a few doubts about my chosen career, this was welcome coverage in more ways than one.

Sir Richard Branson launched Virgin Airlines in a similar fashion. He was then in his twenties, waiting at the airport in Puerto Rico to board a plane to the Virgin Islands, when his flight—the last of the day—was canceled. There weren't enough customers to make it worthwhile for the commercial carrier. But, as Branson would later recall, "I had a beautiful lady waiting for me in BVI." Thus motivated, as well as being supremely annoyed by the lack of consideration for the customers who'd already purchased their tickets, Branson walked over to a charter company and hired a plane that he couldn't afford. In other words, he got ahead of himself. *Then*, he borrowed a chalkboard and wrote "Virgin Airlines" over "$39 one way to BVI." He made the rounds to all the other passengers who'd been bumped. Within minutes, he'd filled up his first plane.[21]

A young executive named Tristan Walker used the same technique when pursuing a job at the nascent company Foursquare. After emailing eight times, Walker finally convinced CEO Dennis Crowley to agree to a sit-down "the next time Tristan was in NYC." Walker immediately replied that he had plans to be in New York the next day. He thus secured an in-person meeting at the Foursquare office. Only *then* did he book an early morning flight from California to New York to fulfill the illusion. Not only was he hired, but he went on to become Foursquare's director of business development.

By reverse-engineering the usual sequence of time in small ways and large, Tristan Walker, Richard Branson, and I all got more than a few steps ahead. One word of caution, however. As with all tricks of illusion, the key to pulling this off is having both full confidence and sufficient command to actually catch up in time.

A nother aspect of magic that plays with time is awe. We all know that when an illusionist pulls off a truly confounding trick, audiences are awestruck. But what does that mean? They raise their eyebrows, drop their jaws, widen their eyes, and gasp. They're surprised, impressed, intimidated, elated, unable to fathom how the effect was created—and while they're mentally suspended in these roiling responses, their perception of time slows down. Their thoughts cascade. Their brains go wild, making memories of each moment's observation while striving to make sense of the impossible thing they've just witnessed.

This may seem like an effect with limited applications, but it turns out that awe is a much more useful—and available—tool than you might think. That's because awe is really all about power.

Researchers Dacher Keltner and Jonathan Haidt define awe as the feeling we experience when confronted by something—or someone—so vastly impressive that we feel both dwarfed by comparison *and* forced to change our assumptions about the world around us. In this sense, it's related to fear, so it makes sense that some of our responses to awe are similar to the effects of fear.

Keltner and Haidt speculate that the sense of awe evolved in humans to ensure that low-rank individuals would submit to superior, more powerful (and often fearsome) leaders who could boost the tribe's chances of survival.[22] This had the effect of maintaining hierarchical order in early societies. Then, as awe developed in response to vast natural beauty, supernatural mysteries, and man-made wonders, it played directly into the hands of sorcerers, high priests, and kings who trafficked in illusions of grandiosity and superior leadership skills. It still does. Today's cult leaders engineer awe to attract followers, as do larger-than-life celebrities, politicians, and dictators.

The surprising thing about awe is, it's not at all difficult to arouse. Advertisers can inspire awe with videos of hikers approaching the summit of an Alpine mountain. A majestic piece of symphonic music will arouse awe. So will a life-size replica of a *Tyrannosaurus rex* skeleton. The triggers in one set of experiments ranged from a sixty-second commercial showing waterfalls, whales, and astronauts in space, to a short story about ascending to the top of the Eiffel Tower and looking out over Paris.[23] A control group was shown a cheerful-but-not-awesome commercial of happy people in a parade, or asked to read about climbing an unnamed tower to look at a nondescript landscape. After watching the video or reading the story, participants were given a set of questions about their sense of time. Compared to the happy or neutral groups, people who'd been briefly (and artificially) awed said they had more time to get things done and were less stressed about time. They felt less impatient and more satisfied with life. And perhaps because they felt less pressed for time, the awestruck group also showed more willingness to spend money for time-intensive events, such as a movie or Broadway show, dinner out, or a massage, instead of buying material goods such as watches or clothes.

So awe sells experience by creating the illusion that people have more time to spend. Useful information if you're marketing an airline or restaurant chain or theme park. But there's an additional layer to all this.

Just as fear makes us hyperalert and creates the illusion that time has slowed down, awe creates a magical suspension of disbelief during which we're acutely aware of what's happening—but are too amazed to ask why. Immediately *after* we emerge from the emotional frames of fear and awe, however, our critical faculties go into overdrive to figure out what just happened and how we need to respond. Just think of the intense conversations that occur as an audience is leaving a world-class magic show. Having been primed with awe, people become more curious, thoughtful, and focused.

SPELLBOUND

Moreover, they'll turn this enhanced attentiveness to *any* problem that surfaces in the aftermath of awe.

Students in one 2010 experiment were shown an awe-inspiring panoramic vista, then asked to evaluate an academic proposal. Compared to students who hadn't seen the vista, the awestruck group spent more time on their analysis, delved more deeply into the arguments for and against, and considered specific content more than the general overview. This suggests that one's frame of attention both sharpens and deepens after a dose of awe—which also gives magicians a strong incentive to save their most awesome acts for last!

One last side effect connects to both the perception of time and the grandeur associated with awe. People become less egotistical, at least for a short time, after being awestruck. And again, it doesn't take much to prime them. One researcher took a group of students to stand in a grove of soaring eucalyptus trees on his University of California campus. He told half of them to look up and the other half to look at a nearby building. Then the researcher began to move past the students but tripped and dropped a bunch of pens he'd been holding. The students who'd reported feeling awed by the trees sprang to his assistance and collected more of the pens than those who'd been staring at the building.

In keeping with the theory that awe evolved to ensure that followers would line up behind leaders, research like this suggests that people who've been filled with awe shift their focus away from themselves, becoming more interested in the larger universe and, feeling less pressed for time, more likely to *spend* time helping and connecting with others. This may explain why churches and synagogues typically offer social events after awe-inspiring sermons and music, and why they're often hubs for community activism. It's also why live audiences who've been dazzled by the awe-inspiring presence and rhetoric of political candidates are more likely to volunteer for their campaigns than are people who merely read about the candidates' policies in the news. In this respect, the power of awe is no illusion, but is an essential game-changer.

5

DESIGN FREE CHOICE

In the opening scene of *Now You See Me,* Jesse Eisenberg's character, a rogue magician, performs a sleight-of-hand trick before a crowd on the streets of Chicago. Simple stuff, except that I wanted to make sure the illusion would involve—and awe—the movie's *viewers* as well as the characters on the screen. So we arranged for Eisenberg to riffle through a deck of cards while staring directly into the camera and asking a girl in the crowd—and, implicitly, the movie audience—to choose one of the cards. The girl picks the seven of diamonds. And so, as it happens, does everyone who watches the film. Then, as Eisenberg tosses the cards in the air, an enormous seven of diamonds is illuminated on the side of a high-rise in the background . . . and viewers of the film are dumbfounded. *But how,* they wonder, *could he possibly have known what card* I *would pick?*

The illusion, of course, is that the audience was choosing freely. Magicians use all sorts of techniques to direct people's thoughts and decisions toward a preordained choice, but the desired effect is only achieved if the audience truly believes that *they* control the outcome. In other words, a magician's goal is to convince his volunteers that they have the freedom to choose, when they in fact do not.

Imagine that I ask you to color a drawing on a pad of paper. With an array of available markers, you freely choose to shade the horse blue. You color the donkey red. Then you decide to make the rooster green. And before you even put down your last marker, I turn over an identical drawing that I colored before the show—revealing the same exact color preferences. *Wow!* How could I have known what choices you'd make? At this point, you're hooked and will closely follow whatever I do next.

Tricks that hinge on audience choices engage spectators much more directly than illusions that are purely objective spectacles. They dissolve the invisible barrier, or fourth wall, that separates the stage from the reality, and everyone in the audience—not just the actual volunteers—feels like a participant in the magic. After all, any of them might be picked next. The result of this dynamic is a win-win—engaging entertainment for you, and more business for me.

The illusion of free choice confers equally potent benefits in other businesses. If your client believes it's *his* idea to buy the product or program you're offering, he's going to be much more receptive than if you strong-arm him through a hard sell. He'll also be more emotionally invested in the future of your brand. And if his choice happens to solve a problem of *yours*, so much the better. The upshot is that *he* will take ownership of the outcome that best serves *your* interests.

BUT YOU ARE FREE TO CHOOSE

In 2000 a couple of French behavioral scientists, Nicolas Guéguen and Alexandre Pascual, conducted a landmark experiment that proved just how potent a business tool the mere *suggestion* of choice can be. They sent a young man to a mall to approach random shoppers with one of two appeals. To the first group he said, "Excuse me, could I ask for some change to take the bus, please?" Just 10 percent of those who received this pitch chose to give him money.

Then he approached a second random group of strangers with the identical appeal, except that he added, "But you are free to accept or refuse." This simple acknowledgment of their free choice pushed his success rate up to 47.5 percent—a nearly *fivefold increase*. What's more, the donors who responded to "But you are free . . ." gave, on average, twice as much.[1]

The researchers wondered if elements of guilt or pity might be influencing these initial results, since the young man was acting as if he needed a charitable favor. So two years later Guéguen and Pascual tweaked their experiment to a more businesslike model, replacing the plea for cash with a request to fill out a standard consumer survey. This time the reminder that participants were free to choose boosted the compliance rate by a more modest but still impressive 15 percent, up from 75.6 percent to 90.1 percent. And today more than forty-two other studies, involving more than 22,000 participants, have confirmed Guéguen and Pascual's core discovery: When people are told they are free, they become more cooperative, more obliging, and more generous. On average, across all these experiments, those four magic little words, ". . . but you are free," doubled compliance rates.

We humans clearly love the idea that we are free to choose how we think and act—so much so that we'll reward a total stranger just for telling us we're free. At the same time, however, we're exquisitely susceptible to suggestions that we are either more, or less, free than we in fact may be. And some of these suggestions we impose on ourselves.

Just think how often you say, hear, or think the phrase "I have to . . ." As if choice is not an option. In fact, choice is always an option. If you're enslaved, incarcerated, or live under a dictatorship, certain choices may have dire consequences, but even in those circumstances you have the option of risking the consequences. So, what's really going on when we say that we "have no choice" is that we're deactivating our sense of personal agency. We're relegating our responsibility for the decision, thus turning what might have been an active choice into a passive one.

For many of us, passive choices make up the bulk of our days. As soon as we arrive at work we turn on the computer, perhaps reflexively, and check email. When the phone rings, we answer. If a colleague suggests lunch, we go along. At the appointed time we get in the car and head home by the usual route for our usual evening routine. These and other passive choices are like mental shortcuts. They're habitual, automatic, intuitive, and they require minimal time and effort. We don't give them any real thought, much less take pleasure or pride in them. But any and all of these choices can *become* active—and more rewarding—through the addition of focus, logic, and deliberation.[2]

Balaji Prabhakar, a Stanford computer scientist and native of Bangalore, India, saw the potential for transforming passive choices into active ones when he helped the IT company Infosys deal with the problem of grueling daily commutes that were eating into employees' work schedules and morale. Prabhakar designed a voluntary program that rewarded workers who clocked in before rush hour by giving them points toward a weekly lottery for cash prizes. He didn't tell them about the underlying problem that *he* was trying to solve, nor did he tell them how to reorganize their daily commutes; he just gave them an incentive to get focused on coming to work earlier, by whatever means *they* chose.[3]

This was the same approach advocated by World War II general George S. Patton, who said, "Never tell people how to do things. Tell them what to do and they will surprise you with their ingenuity." By presenting the puzzle as a personal and engaging game, Prabhakar got the employees fired up to find their own solutions. Within six months the number of Infosys commuters who arrived before eight thirty in the morning had doubled, and the duration of the average commute had dropped by more than 16 percent. Stress levels fell, and company morale rose. Prabhakar had unlocked the power of proactive choice by encouraging the Infosys workers to take ownership of the outcome that best served *his* purposes.

CHOICE ARCHITECTURE

Prabhakar is what behavioral economists Richard Thaler and Cass Sunstein, in their book *Nudge*, call a "choice architect": He designs ways to help "people make choices that they themselves think are better."[4] This approach to leadership is analogous to architecture that encourages the occupants of a house to live more comfortably, productively, and happily—without necessarily being aware of the ways the architect has influenced their behavior. Or, as Dwight D. Eisenhower put it, "Leadership is the art of getting people to want what must be done."

Let's return to the notion of the gap: the space that exists between *perception* of a situation or problem, and *conception* of a response or solution. It is in this shadowy void that both illusionists and choice architects operate, invisibly bridging gaps *for* the audience and projecting conclusions into their brains. The goal is to influence their decisions without directly dictating their actions.

Like all choice architects, magicians govern the gap by reorganizing the context in which audience members make their decisions. Take for example this simple card trick:

- I'll ask you to freely choose a playing card and reinsert it into the deck.
- Then I shuffle and cut the cards, place four cards face-down in a line on the table, and ask you to turn over one of these four.
- To your astonishment, the card you *yourself* turn over will be the same card you initially chose from the pack.

All the choices were yours, yet I've directed the outcome by tracking the card you first chose and making sure it was placed second away from you in that lineup of four. Odds were, you'd avoid the first card because it was too obvious a choice, and I positioned the third and fourth cards just far enough away that they'd require you physically to lean forward in order to touch them. Even that slight effort was enough to deter you, leaving the second position as your natural pick. Thus, by altering your *choice environment*—or context—I nudged you toward my intended outcome. And you were all the more amazed because you had total freedom.

While magicians nudge for the sake of entertainment, choice architects like Balaji Prabhakar are working to solve more pragmatic problems in companies, public policy, and governments all over the world. In 2010, for example, Great Britain established its own sixty-person "nudge unit," officially known as the Behavioral

Insights Team. Think MI-6, but instead of "00 agents," the team is composed of policy makers who are licensed to nudge.

One of the problems BIT took on was Britain's high rate of delinquent income tax payments. To nudge people to pay up, the team sent debtors letters informing them that the majority of people in their community had paid their taxes on time. A second letter pointed out that most people in their tax bracket had already paid. A third, which proved the most effective, included both statements. In 2012, this campaign netted £210 million of tax revenue that would otherwise have required lengthy and expensive collection procedures.[5]

Choice architects may change the context by altering the audience's perception of the problem. The British nudge unit did this by converting the debtors' concept of their tax problem from legal obligation to a more personal social concern. The campaign's success is explained by people paying up to avoid social disgrace, a problem very different than the one that their choice was solving for the British government. Herein lies the illusion.

Choice and problems go together like hens and eggs. You can't have one without the other, but which comes first? Ordinarily, we think of problems preceding—and demanding—choices. But choice architects understand that this order is not always as it appears. Sometimes it takes a decoy problem, like imminent social disgrace, to generate choices that will solve the true problem.

Other times it makes sense to present an array of attractive choices as "opportunities" without even mentioning the underlying problem. I do this all the time in my shows, asking audience members at random to pick a card, or color, or word, thus piquing their curiosity about my purpose and holding their attention until I *later* reveal the puzzle their choices have "solved."

————————→   DESIGN FREE CHOICE

The Denver-based tech company FullContact uses a similar strategy when it makes new employees an offer that seems too good to refuse: They'll receive $7,500 on top of their basic salary if only they'll choose to take time off from work. The illusion is that this is purely for their own good. The contact management software company calls these initiatives "paid paid vacations." The catch? The incentive only kicks in if employees promise to completely unplug during these holidays—no emails, texts, no calls. According to communications director Brad McCarty, "If you are on the grid and working and get caught, you have to pay it back. That's the agreement." In management's eyes, the program works spectacularly. Nearly every single employee has opted to unplug, thus solving a serious problem the company had been having with talent retention in the highly competitive tech market. Unplugged vacations resulted in increased company morale and a stronger work-life balance. By choosing to accept the offer, new hires helped to solve problems they didn't know existed.[6]

Even when they don't reveal the ulterior problem, however, choice architects work hard to give choosers a sense of participation and satisfaction in their decisions. Active, not passive, choices are the preferred goal. I apply the same principle in my shows by packaging questions as clever quizzes. I might ask for a four-letter word for the pun "picked locks," which will get the whole audience competing. Even after one savvy solver shouts out, "AFRO!" everyone else will be primed and ready to play the next puzzle—and they'll be paying close attention to me. My hope is that, as the audience spills out into the lobby after the show, they'll feel smart and accomplished—and also more connected to the shared experience of my performance.

Wipro BPO, a division of the business process outsourcing firm Wipro, found that a similar approach helped reduce employee burnout. The underlying problem seemed to be a failure of the existing training program to cultivate individual enthusiasm or loyalty for the company. But this changed dramatically when new hires were invited during orientation to consider ways that they could apply their personal strengths to their work at Wipro. The resulting sense of individual empowerment and proactive agency created an emotional bond with the organization. Once this training approach was adopted, Wipro BPO saw not only lower rates of turnover, but also higher rates of customer satisfaction with employee performance.[7]

PULLING THE STRINGS OF CHOICE

Choice architects exploit several basic human tendencies when devising their motivational approaches. With the British income tax debtors, BIT tapped into the "bandwagon effect": No matter how independent we may believe ourselves to be, humans at the core are social creatures, so we're profoundly influenced by the attitudes, beliefs, and choices of others, especially within our own community or "tribe." Most of us crave the security of belonging—and dread the shame of being outcasts. So the British nudge unit employed the power of peer pressure by subtly framing responsible tax payment as a basic cost of belonging to a desired class.

BIT counted on a related bias, called "loss aversion," when designing a plan to collect delinquent vehicle taxes. Researchers have found that our dread of losing something is twice as potent as our pleasure over winning the exact same thing. So the threat of a tangible loss is a much stronger motivator than the promise of a reward. With this in mind, the nudge unit sent scofflaws the message, "Pay your tax or lose your car," and included a picture of the car in jeopardy. These letters increased payment rates by 20 percent.[8]

Another factor in choice architecture is "choice support" bias, which means that, once we've made a decision, we "own" it and will generally defend it, right or wrong—even if it's proven to be a mistake. We'll play up its positive aspects and minimize—or ignore—its negative consequences. In effect, we treat our choices as extensions of ourselves.

This particular tendency proved extremely useful to the FBI's choice architect, Gary Noesner, early in the 1993 siege at the Branch Davidian compound in Waco, Texas. At the time, cult leader David Koresh was hunkered down with a cache of illegal weapons; and more than one hundred followers, including several dozen children, were trapped with him in the compound. After Koresh fired on approaching agents from the Bureau of Alcohol, Tobacco, and Firearms, the FBI was called in to try to negotiate an end to the standoff. Noesner's first objective was to secure the release of the children.

He knew that Koresh had said at the outset of the siege that his followers were free to leave. Before anyone actually could get out of the compound, the cult leader changed his mind, and yet, Noesner told me, "In a strange way he had problems going back on his word." So Noesner kept reminding Koresh of his own free choice to let his people go, if they wished.

"'David,' he'd say, "'as you said to us so many times, people are free to make the choices that they want.'" By preserving Koresh's illusion of autonomy, by allowing him to own his *own* choices, Noesner enabled him to feel he was determining the fate of those he released from the compound. And in doing so, Noesner could save lives.

In his early days at the FBI Academy in Quantico, Virginia, Noesner had drafted an extensive handbook that trained negotiators to actively listen, exhibit empathy, and attempt to understand the individual on the other side of the situation. In Waco, he put these tactics to the test, and over the first twenty-six days his team negotiated the release of thirty-five hostages, including nineteen children.

Unfortunately, Noesner's negotiating team was a subordinate unit, overrun by bureaucracy and not formally designated. There was tension between the tactical unit, who wanted to go in with guns blazing, and the negotiators, who wanted to continue with Noesner's approach. The tactical commanders did not acknowledge the incremental progress the choice architects were making. Frustrated that they had not received absolute surrender, they wanted to punish Koresh for his hubris and defiance. As FBI commander Jeff Jamar readied the tear gas, Noesner was taken off the case.

The debacle that ensued would be watched on television by millions. Instead of exploiting the gap in Koresh's perceptions, the FBI literally bulldozed it. When their armored vehicles began slamming through the walls, Koresh set the compound ablaze. Only nine Davidians staggered out of the flames. Seventy-five bodies were found in the ashes, including Koresh's.

Forced to acknowledge their tactical mistake, the FBI subsequently created a full negotiation program, called the Crisis Negotiation Unit. Noesner would spend the next ten years, until his retirement, as its chief. When I caught up with him recently, he explained that choice is a central element of all negotiations.

⟶   **DESIGN FREE CHOICE**

"Make decisions *with* your opponent," he advised. Ultimatums don't work, but questions often do. For instance, say the hostage taker is hungry. The negotiator involves him in his own solution by asking, "'What are your thoughts on how to get some food in to you?' If he happens to say something that is agreeable—it's *his* idea. If it's unacceptable: 'Let's see if we can come up with some ideas . . . let's work together to make this happen.'"

In his book *Stalling for Time: My Life as an FBI Hostage Negotiator*, Noesner explains, "People want to be shown respect, and they want to be understood. . . . The positive relationship achieved through this interaction then sets the stage for the negotiator to exert a positive influence over others' behavior, steering them away from violence."

This is choice architecture in action.

FIND THE LADY

Visit a tourist site in any major city and you're bound to come across a "dealer" mixing up three lengthwise folded cards on an upside-down cardboard box. One of the most common confidence games, three-card monte (also called the three-card trick or Find the Lady) has existed since at least the mid-nineteenth century. Robert-Houdin's writing about "Les Trois Cartes" in 1861 is one of the earliest records of the scam.

The game is simple: One of the cards, usually a queen, is the target. The other two are different, often aces. The three cards are mixed up and the player has to find the queen, the "money card."

A variety of sleights are used to manipulate the cards, but one of the dealer's most effective techniques is known as "the bent corner move." During the mixing of the cards, the dealer "accidently" bends one of the corners of the money card, making it more discernible to the player. The dealer pretends to be oblivious to this, often allowing confederate participants ("shills") to win money. But after the player places his bet, the dealer, in the course of shuffling the cards, deftly straightens out the corner and bends up the corner of *another* card.

Feeling privy to secret information, the player will assuredly choose the card with the bent corner, not the queen, thereby losing his bet.

It's human nature. The con man knows that we take ownership over the things we discover ourselves.

CHOICE OVERLOAD

Ironically, choice architects generally succeed by limiting the number of choices on offer. In other words, freedom of choice actually *needs* to be an illusion for choice to work as a motivational tool. Why? Because having too many options can so overwhelm people that they're unable to make any decision at all. It may also

———————→   DESIGN FREE CHOICE

make them less certain about the selection they do ultimately choose.

Think about it. We all like the *idea* of infinite possibilities, but when confronted with a limitless array, how do you choose? At Portland's Loyal Legion bar, you're confronted with a mind-boggling ninety-nine Oregon brewed beers on tap. Do you order one of twenty IPAs? Or one of the fifteen Oakshire beers? How about those eleven new Oregon craft ciders? And how long will it take you to make up your mind? Will you then savor your pick, or rush through it to try another?

The effects of choice overload also dominate the world of online dating. Paul Eastwick, an assistant professor of human development at the University of Texas at Austin who studies romantic relationships, has found that by presenting so many constantly changing potential partners, Tinder, OkCupid, and other dating apps actually can reduce the chances of romantic commitment.

The problem here is what social scientist Barry Schwartz calls "the paradox of choice." When we're constantly bombarded with new prospects, we naturally think that a more attractive, smarter, richer, sexier possibility might turn up at any minute. For many dating app users, this makes it all but impossible to choose a mate for keeps.[9]

Magicians, like other choice architects, use a variety of tactics to get around this paradox, while still maximizing the positive effects of choice. For instance, when I call on volunteers to pick a card, I'll often limit their "time window" to a few seconds, so they won't have a chance to second-guess their decisions. Casinos do the same thing at gaming tables, forcing players to choose their bets fast and take their chances.

Businesses use an equivalent tactic when offering sale discounts "for a limited time only." The idea is to motivate the consumer to push away competing distractions and commit to a final choice *now*. So Macy's will offer "4 Day Specials!" Amazon has created "Deals of the Day." And for thirty-three years, Toyota has packed consumer incentives into annual "Toyotathons," limited to the Christmas season.

Another strategy to defuse choice overload is to present a default option. When people feel overwhelmed by too many possibilities, they almost always go for the one that's most familiar or easiest to access. That ready choice is the default option.

In business, defaults are often the passive choices a consumer makes by doing little or nothing. Opt-out systems for retirement contributions, for example, require no active effort on the part of employees who want a percentage of their paychecks to go directly into their IRA; only those who *don't* want to participate need take action. Researchers have found that 90 percent or more of employees elect to make automatic contributions when that's the default choice. By comparison, in companies that require an active sign-up to opt *in* to a retirement plan, only about half of workers participate.[10]

As Richard Thaler puts it, "Default options are sticky." In other words, because they require the least effort, they have an excellent chance of being selected. But this means, he warns, "[i]f you are the choice architect, you need to spend a lot of time thinking about what those default options should be."[11]

"FORCING" THE ILLUSION OF FREE CHOICE

In the opening of *Now You See Me* the seven of diamonds is the default choice because it's (secretly) the only choice. As Jesse Eisenberg flips his card deck, the audience assumes that fifty-two different choices are flashing before their eyes, but only one is clearly discernible. The rest fly by too quickly to register. This tactic is called a force, and it's one of an illusionist's most essential tools.

In some forces, the magician makes sure only one item can be selected. In others, he offers a variety of defaults, any one of which will serve his purposes. Imagine a dozen books spread out on a table. You see they are of various shapes, sizes, and colors. The titles are different. The authors are different. You conclude that all is fair. But maybe the magician has replaced *every single page* of each book so that they are all identical. It's much easier now for the magician to figure out what paragraph you'll select, right? He's prepared for whatever you "freely" choose.

In his work, Gary Noesner calls this type of force the "alternate choice method." He would use it during hostage negotiations to provide the opposition with multiple choices—but only one outcome. In 1988, for example, a mentally unstable man named Charlie Leaf had kidnapped his ex-wife and four-year-old son and held them hostage at gunpoint in a Virginia farmhouse. After a sleepless night of negotiating, Noesner finally convinced Leaf to exit the farmhouse by promising him and his captives safe transport on a helicopter. But he had to make sure Leaf did *not* come out the rear of the house, because that's where the SWAT team was clustered. Noesner wanted to avoid an unpredictable shootout and get Leaf out in the open where marksmen could neutralize him. So he provided Leaf with several choices and the illusion of control: "Would you like to leave from the front door, the side door, or through one of the windows?" Even though Leaf had his child strapped to his shoulders and his wife gripped tightly in front of him, the sharpshooters were able to take him down. Noesner's force saved the lives of Leaf's wife and child.

SPELLBOUND

MAGICIAN'S CHOICE

If I want to force your selection from an array of objects, I can use a tactic called "magician's choice," and you'll believe you've chosen freely. The secret is that I adjust my responses to your decisions in ways that will lead you to think that you've chosen the forced item.

Let's say I've placed two coins on the table, a quarter and a half dollar, and I want you to pick the half dollar. I'll ask you to choose one of the coins and hand it to me. If you select the half dollar, I silently thank you because no force is needed.

But if you hand me the quarter, I'll put that coin away and reframe the half dollar that you *left* on the table as "your choice," then swiftly move on with the rest of the trick before you can second-guess me.

Variations of this tactic can also be used with larger numbers of objects. It just takes confidence and finesse. The key is to act quickly and decisively, so it appears as if the "rules" that produce the forced choice were in play from the very beginning.

The ethics of forcing in business, of course, are more complicated. When is it okay to limit a consumer's choices? Or to manipulate consumer behavior to comply with a company's goals? True forcing, in which a single outcome is unequivocally foisted on the consumer, best describes the practices of a monopoly or a cartel. But a different way to think about forcing in business is to frame it

---------------->   DESIGN FREE CHOICE

as a strategy that focuses the consumer's attention on a target range of choices.

Coca-Cola uses the alternate choice force to stack the odds of your buying one of its products every time you shop the beverage aisle in your local supermarket. The exact brands may vary depending on where you live, but you'll likely find the shelves stocked with Dr Pepper, Fanta, Fresca, Pibb Xtra, Schweppes, Sprite, TaB, Dasani, Evian, at least five varieties of Coke, five varieties of Glaceau waters, six varieties of Minute Maid juice drinks, Odwalla juices, Fuze teas, Five Alive, Powerade, Zico coconut water . . . a veritable cornucopia of choices. Right? Well, yes and no. These different brands do represent distinctive products that appeal to a wide variety of consumer preferences. But in economic terms, that variety of choice is illusory because all of these brands belong to Coca-Cola. So if you think your purchasing power is supporting a natural juice manufacturer when you buy Odwalla, think again. Coca-Cola here is like a master magician using the illusion of variety to the advantage of his bottom line.

Designers of retail malls and markets also employ forces. Since all retail shopping environments are essentially choice emporiums, the task of those who design these spaces is to make sure each shopper is exposed to as many of the emporium's offerings as possible, but in a slow, controlled way that doesn't trigger choice overload. To this end, the location of escalators in most malls forces customers to stroll past an entire floor of shops before moving to the next level. And elevators, which bypass this force, are often strategically located in hard-to-find nooks and corners. The net result is that many shoppers will spend extra time at the mall—and be exposed to many more retail choices than they would if the escalators were close together.

SPELLBOUND

But the forces in the average mall pale by comparison with those of the home-furnishing superstore IKEA. Although the exit in most IKEA stores is adjacent to the entrance, the two portals are typically separated by a barrier of affordable armoires and cabinets, so shoppers are forced into a maze of home furnishings that leads them literally thousands of feet to end up inches from where they began. The effect is so disorienting that consumers often lose sight of their original shopping targets. As they wander past colorful stacks of kitchenware, hardware, bedding, and bath toys, they're a captive audience for impulse temptations. As Alan Penn, of the Virtual Reality Centre for the Built Environment at University College London, explains, "Here the trick is that because the layout is so confusing you know you won't be able to go back and get it later, so you pop it in your trolley as you go past."[12]

Of all the commercial forces, however, perhaps none is as controversial as the proprietary jacks on Apple products. The iPhone 7, like earlier models, has a nonstandard earphone port, but this one only takes the new Lightning connector. Not only do the plugins for other brands of phones not work with it, but all accessories for past iPhones are useless, as well. Of course, Apple makes the case that the new port is smaller and more versatile, a technological improvement, but the bottom line for consumers is that each upgrade will force them to replace all their iPhone accessories— adding profits for Apple and forcing out competing accessory manufacturers.

Not surprisingly, the coercive aspect of Apple's force has generated a bit of a backlash from resentful consumers. "Apple is about to rip off every one of its customers," reads the complaint on the social activism site SumOfUs. "Again," it adds. Irate at the added expense being foisted upon them, not to mention all that electronic waste, nearly a quarter of a million people signed the protest petition in early January 2016.[13]

The flaw in Apple's approach is that it fails to create the illusion that the choice was the customer's own. Instead, consumers *feel* the force of the company's will. This is a mistake that no seasoned magician would make.

THE POWER OF THE LEAVE-BEHIND

To see how the illusion of choice can be reverse-engineered, let's travel back in time. It's World War II. April 30, 1943, to be exact. A local fisherman off the coast of Huelva, Spain, discovers a decomposing body floating in the Atlantic. The corpse is facedown, kept afloat by a life jacket, and dressed in military khakis. Chained to his wrist is a black briefcase. The contents of his wallet identify him as Major William Martin, of the Royal British Marines. A postmortem concludes that the man fell into the sea while still alive, and that his body has been floating in the sea between three and five days.

Except that Major William Martin is an illusion, a fictional character invented by a team of hush-hush members of Section 17M, the most secret wartime branch of the British Secret Service, as part of an elaborate—and critically important—disinformation mission labeled Operation Mincemeat.

Major Martin's briefcase contains false information that suggests the Allies are planning to invade Greece and Sardinia in 1943. Even though Spain is a neutral country, much of its military sides with Hitler, and the Mincemeat masterminds have calculated that news of the mysterious Major Martin will swiftly wend its way to Berlin. The German high command has long suspected that the Allies will launch an attack across the Mediterranean from North Africa, but they have no way of knowing whether the landing will occur in Greece and Sardinia, Sicily, or the Balkans. The documents in Martin's briefcase plant just enough clues so that after the Germans solve the riddle of Major Martin they will choose to concentrate their own defenses in Greece and Sardinia.

Which will leave the Allies free to land with minimal opposition in *Sicily* on July 10, 1943.

And that's just what happened. In magician-speak, Major Martin was a "false leave-behind" that helped the Allies win the war.

T he false leave-behind is one of the most powerful weapons in a magician's arsenal. If used deftly, it can make an illusion unbreakable because, if your audience members, or say, the Germans, discover something themselves, they won't need to be forced to believe in it. Instead, they'll make this choice of their own genuinely free will.

Even in the simplest of tricks, doubtful audiences can be converted into true believers when a false leave-behind is deployed. Let's say an audience member decides on his own to investigate one of my tricks after a show and discovers "objective evidence" that "proves" I performed an impossible feat. As soon as he makes this discovery, my illusion becomes ironclad. For this reason, the leave-behind is often built into the act.

Consider the "blow book," one of the oldest and simplest of all manufactured magic props. The name originates from the practice of sixteenth-century showmen asking spectators to blow on a blank

book, which then filled magically with colorful drawings. Today, the most widely used blow book is the *Magic Coloring Book*, a staple of children's birthday party shows. Most adults quickly figure out the device: The book's pages are cut like a fashion magazine's so that the magician can flip to certain sections, revealing either blank, black-and-white, or colored pages. But with a little extra effort, the magician can transform this basic trick into a head-scratching mystery. For $4.95 at hocus-pocus.com a magician can purchase an *all-blank* version of the *Magic Coloring Book*. Then, after the show, that blank book is "forgotten" on a table at the party. Even the most skeptical parent who finds this book will have second thoughts, and the child who finds it will definitely believe in magic!

Leave-behinds work almost entirely because of choice-supportive bias: We feel more ownership and excitement over the ideas we arrive at on our own. In recent years, hip marketing companies have harnessed this principle to create leave-behinds with mesmerizing effects on consumers.

One such campaign was designed by the innovative "active engagement" agency 42 Entertainment to engineer advance excitement in 2007 for the Nine Inch Nails album *Year Zero*. It started in a bathroom stall at a NIN concert in Lisbon, Portugal, where a fan discovered a USB drive containing an unprotected MP3 of NIN's yet-to-be-released song "My Violent Heart." Other USB drives turned up in Barcelona, Spain, and Manchester, England, containing more tracks from the unreleased album. The lucky finders kicked off a flurry of online buzz about the album and the band. Fans posted MP3s to their websites and lit up the message boards with their theories about the source of these "illegal" leaks.

SPELLBOUND

Simultaneously, fans were discovering secret codes in the T-shirts purchased at NIN concerts. Highlighted letters on one shirt spelled out the lyrics "I am trying to believe." When fans added a ".com" and looked online, they found themselves in a dystopian website keyed to the content of the album. Another tour T-shirt code yielded a phone number. When curious fans dialed it, they heard a bit of the album's lead single, "Survivalism." That song quickly shot up to number two on the airplay-based Modern Rock chart.[14]

Why do these leave-behind tactics work so well? The answer can be found on 42 Entertainment's website: "Audiences are primed for discovery. . . . When you give people new things to discover, not only will they spread it through their networks but it becomes their own."[15] Major Martin couldn't agree more.

EMPLOY THE FAMILIAR

Late in the summer of 1942, after the first battle of El Alamein halted in a draw, the Allies' Eighth Army forces in Egypt and Rommel's Axis Afrika Korps found themselves in a standoff. The grueling, monthlong battle had worn down troops on both sides and left First Marshal Rommel, the notorious "Desert Fox" who'd pushed the Allies from Tripoli to Cairo, too ill to hold command. British prime minister Winston Churchill sent in the "Spartan general," Bernard Montgomery, to break the stalemate with a decisive Allied victory. Montgomery, however, was keenly aware that the standard patterns of warfare, even with the Allies' now superior air and arms power, wouldn't do the trick. So he called in the Camouflage squad.

Led by veteran film director Geoffrey Barkas, the Camouflage Development and Training Centre (CDTC) included legendary magician Jasper Maskelyne and a team of professional painters, sculptors, and architects. Since its inception in 1940, the CDTC's mission had been to fulfill for the Allies the battlefield mandate first articulated by Sun Tzu in the fifth century BC: "When we are able to attack, we must seem unable; when using our forces, we must appear inactive; when we are near, we must make the enemy believe we are far away; when far away, we must make him believe we are near." In other words, the artists' mission was to turn the Germans' assumptions against them.

The CDTC's previous coup, at the siege of Tobruk in Libya, had been to protect a vital desalination plant by making it look as if enemy bombers had already destroyed it. In Egypt, their sleights had three far larger goals:

- To conceal the Allied troop buildup around the train station in the north of the El Alamein region.
- To make the Allied preparations seem slower than they really were.
- To make General Georg Stumme, Rommel's replacement, think that the British were preparing to attack from the south.

And they had just six short weeks to accomplish all this.

The illusionists started by sizing up the patterns that reconnaissance units use to gauge the enemy's location, size, activities, and intentions. Then they turned those patterns into illusions. They created dummy tanks, field guns, activity, and encampments for two whole phantom divisions to the south of El Alamein. At the same time, they vanished the real tanks and field guns being assembled in the north.

Stage and illusionist props were essential, both to conceal the actual tanks and matériel in the north and to create the illusion of troops massing for action in the south. These devices included a truck-shaped tank cover called a sunshield, invented by Maskelyne. It consisted of fabric and plywood casings that made the tank look, from the air, like an ordinary supply truck and that could be opened up or shed when the disguise was no longer needed. Field guns and the tractors that pulled them were similarly disguised under dummy truck canopies called "cannibals." At the same time, five hundred dummy tanks were made from calico-covered palm-frond frames, which could fit over jeeps for mobility. Boxes of essential supplies were stacked and covered with camouflage nets to resemble trucks in the north, while more than seven hundred dummy stacks of empty matériel boxes and cans and one hundred fifty fake artillery guns were staged in the south.

The team also staged fake arms depots and pipelines to "supply" the south. Faux pipeline crews pantomimed digging ditches and laying "pipes" that consisted of empty gasoline cans. Not only did the route of the two-hundred-mile pipeline misdirect the Germans away from the true battle location, but the slow pace of the diggers also created a false timeline for the Allied battle plans. Meanwhile, British counterintelligence had created a fictitious informant who was feeding the Germans phony intelligence by wireless to bolster the illusion being created on the ground.

Initially the staging included six hundred real tanks positioned in the decoy encampment to the south. They, combined with the pipeline and misinformation operations, told the Germans to relax, the Brits couldn't possibly be ready to attack. Then, on October 21, under cover of night, the Allies made the final moves in the greatest military conjuring trick in history. Right in front of the Axis troops, those real tanks in the south were replaced with dummies, then driven in the guise of convoy trucks fifty miles north.

When the Allied bombardment began on October 23, General Stumme was taken completely by surprise. He thought the attack was still weeks away, *and* he'd diverted half his forces to the south because that's where he thought it would start. The mistake cost him his life. Two weeks later, announcing victory at El Alamein, Churchill said "a word about surprise and strategy":

> By a marvelous system of camouflage, complete tactical surprise was achieved in the desert. . . . The enemy suspected that the attack was impending but did not know how, when or where, and above all he had no idea of the scope upon which he was to be assaulted.[1]

Eisenhower took note and, the following year, began forming a Ghost Army to impersonate U.S. Army units, in order to deceive the enemy in Europe. America's Ghost Army included many artists who would become celebrities after the war, including fashion designer Bill Blass, painter Ellsworth Kelly, and actor Douglas Fairbanks Jr. Although this unit numbered only about 1,000 actual men, their battlefield illusions simulated two divisions, or more than *30,000* ghost troops, to divert the Germans away from actual combat locations.

One Ghost Army company used sound patterns exclusively to convince the Germans that Allied troops were advancing where none actually existed. These sonic deceptions consisted of extensive recordings of armored and infantry troop units, which were amplified from the phantom battle zone so that they could be heard up to fifteen miles away. As one former 3132 Signal Company lieutenant recalled, "We could go in at night and crank the speakers up out of the back of the half-track, and play a program to the enemy all night, of us bringing equipment into the scene. And we could make them believe that we were coming in with an armored division."[2]

SPELLBOUND

Beginning just after D-Day, the Ghost Army staged more than twenty battlefield deceptions. Together with CDTC, these military magicians proved beyond a doubt that pattern illusions play a vital role in the theater of war.

SEEING IN PATTERNS

The original inspiration for military camouflage was nature. From the patterns of design that distinguish one species from another, to the patterns of behavior that allow members within species to communicate with each other, nature endows animals with almost limitless forms of—and opportunities for—protective and predatory illusion. The flounder, for example, can change both its color and *pattern* to match its background, acquiring polka dots or checks in as little as eight seconds, to hide both from its larger predators and from its own unsuspecting meal of shrimp or crabs. The markings on the polyphemus moth resemble the eyes of an owl, an illusion designed by nature to spare the moth from small birds that fear the larger owl, which happily is *too* large to be bothered with a lowly moth. Meanwhile, dozens of birds, from warblers to crows, expertly mimic the alarm or threat calls of enemy species, to scare them away from protected territory, nests, or food supplies. Camouflage is an art of illusion that was mastered in the animal kingdom long before the dawn of humanity.

Naturally, humans, too, are born ready to recognize—and be fooled by—predictable patterns. Scott Johnson at the University of California, Los Angeles's Baby Lab conducted, with colleagues in Italy, an experiment in which forty-eight newborns, between one and three days old, were shown a repeating pattern of black and white shapes (triangles, circles, squares, to name a few) without break or delay between the sequences. The study found that the infants would fixate on these "habituation" patterns, locking on to the repeating sequences until they grew bored and turned away. But as soon as the pattern was changed, interrupted with a shape that altered the pattern, the newborn's gaze returned, demonstrating recognition of a new pattern.[3]

One of the key patterns we're wired to recognize is the symmetrical composition of two eyes above a nose, above a mouth. Just minutes old, newborns will turn toward the faces around them, and those faces don't have to be familiar, or even human, to attract them. Six-month-olds who are shown pictures of individual monkeys quickly become as adept at telling one monkey from another as they are in telling people apart.[4] Adults can't do this, unless they spend a great deal of time around monkeys. But infants are "broadly tuned" to study and distinguish any face they're shown early in life. That includes both monkeys and also people of any race or ethnicity, no matter how different from the baby's own.

The time window for this open-mindedness, however, is pretty brief. Unless they're surrounded by monkeys and extraordinarily diverse family members, the same babies will stop paying close attention to the faces of "others" outside their ethnic circle, and they'll soon lose the ability to read them closely. By the time they're toddlers, all monkeys will basically look alike to them, as will members of foreign races.

This trend, called "perceptual narrowing," explains why white Americans who've had little exposure to Asia tend to think all Chinese, Japanese, and Koreans "look alike"—and vice versa. Early humans, of course, had good reason to quickly identify members of foreign—and likely hostile—tribes as "other," while using more discerning brainpower to distinguish who was who within their own tribe. That's why perceptual narrowing occurs. It can be moderated by exposing babies, children, and ourselves to more diverse communities of friends and neighbors, but it can't simply be wished or scolded away. Our reliance on patterns—and our limited ability to decode them—run way too deep.

One reason we rely on repeating patterns is that they're shortcuts. We instinctively favor familiar faces so that we can read them quickly, without laboring to identify them. Likewise, we favor familiar patterns of action—routines—so that our hand knows exactly where to reach for the soap, or keyboard, or orange juice, or car keys without our needing to think about it.

Consider your own morning pattern. Wake up, get up, shower, dress, coffee, food, brush teeth, car, drive, work. When the routine is automatic, you conserve precious thought and energy for more important concerns, like the board meeting that awaits you once you *get* to the office. It's all about native efficiency.

But there is a downside. Just think of all that you *don't* notice as you move through this familiar pattern. Does your autopilot allow you to make an inspired wardrobe or breakfast choice? Would you notice if someone had broken into your living room overnight and made off with a figurine from the corner? Are you able to fully absorb what your son is telling you over breakfast? The information that falls outside the frame of your routine is the equivalent of the idiosyncratic details in monkey faces that babies stop noticing at nine months—or the seams in the sunshields that the Germans failed to detect in El Alamein. They're right in front of you, but you're blind to them. In this sense, our cognitive dependence on patterns can be our Achilles' heel. And magicians take advantage of this.

EMPLOY THE FAMILIAR

Another way humans use patterns is to organize and make sense of the world. We do this largely by associating patterns with meaning, a process, logically enough, called "association learning."

This sentence, with its letters patterned into the words you're reading, is one example of learned association. A red light blinking above an intersection is another. So is the arrangement of numbers on your credit card or bank statement. Whether they consist of spots on a flounder, or headlights on a car, patterns are patterns because they repeat in a predictable fashion with an associated meaning and purpose.

The big difference between flounder patterns and human patterns lies in their diversity and interpretation. As Cambridge University neuroscientist Daniel Bor explains in *The Ravenous Brain*:

> Perhaps what most distinguishes us humans from the rest of the animal kingdom is our ravenous desire to find structure in the information we pick up in the world. We cannot help actively searching for patterns—any hook in the data that will aid our performance and understanding. We constantly look for regularities in every facet of our lives, and there are few limits to what we can learn and improve on as we make these discoveries. We also develop strategies to further help us—strategies that themselves are forms of patterns that assist us in spotting other patterns.

This passion for patterns expresses itself in the repeating phrases and rhythms of music, in the familiar forms and ratios of composition in art, in the metaphors and analogies that deliver much of the deepest meaning in literature. It dominates mathematics and scientific inquiry, which constantly seek patterns of structure and behavior to explain physical and social phenomena. Indeed, puzzles of all kinds are based on finding and/or creating patterns. They challenge us to make order out of chaos.

The problem, as any sudoku addict knows, is that when we seek patterns, we sometimes find patterns that aren't really there, and we may jump too quickly to assumptions about their meaning. In other words, we see an effect and associate it with the wrong cause.

Ancient tribes observed that the sun rose and set at predictable times each day, and mistakenly concluded that the sun was circling the earth. A gambler at the roulette wheel notices a recurring sequence of numbers, and bets accordingly—and loses. A teacher accuses a student of cheating because of a sudden pattern of successful tests, when the student simply has an aptitude for the particular test material. A doctor misdiagnoses cancer based on a pattern of false positives in the patient's screening results. And audiences throughout history have attributed "supernatural powers" to sorcerers, magicians, and mentalists because of special effects. Belief in illusion is one term for this. Superstition is another.

GAMBLER'S FALLACY

On August 18, 1913, at Le Grand Casino of Monte Carlo, the ball of the roulette wheel landed on black. Then it landed on black again. And again. And again. People started to crowd around the table. Black again. Another black.

And this is when cognitive bias started to kick in. Believing that red was "due," people staked large amounts on red. But black hit an utterly improbable twenty-six consecutive times. By the time the streak finally ended, the casino had made millions, owing entirely to chance.

The losers had the gambler's, or the Monte Carlo, fallacy to blame. Simply put, this fallacy is the denial of randomness. We assume that the universe operates according to predictable rules, which we can use to guide our own responses.

Many of us don't just believe that wins will "balance" out losses; we bank on it. Why? Because our brains have difficulty processing chaos. We need a sense of control, so we instinctively search for order in the form of patterns—even when none exist.

We then use these real or imagined patterns to explain and predict events not in our control. For example, a couple who have several daughters might believe that they are "due" to have a boy. Or the gambler at the slot machine that hasn't paid out in twenty spins will keep playing because, surely, it can't hold out all night.

But you know what? There is no law that guarantees probability. As mathematician Alex Bellos puts it, "True randomness has no memory of what came before." This means that every single coin toss has a 50 percent chance of coming up heads, and the same chance of coming up tails. It makes no difference what result the last toss—or the last seventy—produced.

Bellos advises that we'd all do well to stop ascribing meaning to random occurrences, especially when money's involved. "Keeping the gambler's fallacy in check," he says, "makes good business sense."[5]

Biologists believe there's a good evolutionary reason for superstition.[6] It begins with a process called the "priming effect," which conditions the brain to respond to information according to predictable patterns. The priming effect told early *Homo sapiens* to run and hide whenever they spotted an animal in the pattern of a saber-toothed tiger. That was more common sense than superstition, since the tiger would almost certainly cause terrible effects. But what about the rustling branches that *sometimes* indicated the presence of the tiger? The rustle didn't cause the tiger's attack, but it might be associated with the attack, and that association could give rise to a superstition about the dire events that were bound to occur if a tribesman saw that particular bush rustle. The simple evolutionary explanation for this is, better safe than sorry. If a wariness about that rustle kept people on their toes, the price of a little anxiety and a lot of false alarms was worth it. If the tribe that steered clear of the rustle survived, for whatever real reason, longer than the tribe that ignored it, the fear of the rustle would likely be passed down to the next generation. Only when a superstition was associated with more harm than good—when a potion for heat rash, for instance, proved fatal instead of healing—would the evolutionary odds turn sharply against it.

Most magicians, of course, rely on garden-variety associations, aka assumptions, rather than elaborate superstitions, to pull off their tricks. These assumptions pepper our days, so many of them and so frequent that we take them for granted. We neither question them nor need them explained, because all are the product of our own personal scientific method since birth, a process called habituation. From the time we're babies, we observe patterns of design and behavior around us, and notice their purpose or effect, and when that association between pattern and effect is consistent, we record the linkage as fact.

Fact: That chirping sound you hear means there's a bird nearby.

Fact: When I drop a ball, it falls downward.

Fact: Coins make a clinking sound when I shake them in my palm. So if I plan to use this pattern in an illusion, I'll habituate the audience to it by loudly jingling a couple of coins during on-beats early in the show. Then, once the pattern is secure, I'll create the clinking sound *without* actually dropping the coin, thus using sound misdirection to create the illusion that I hold two coins in my hand when I now only have one. This is exactly the strategy that the Ghost Army's 3132 Signal Service Company used in World War II.

Visual habituation shapes our assumptions even about static objects. We see a familiar pattern and, at a glance, we identify it. Let's say there's a stack of ten books onstage. You'll assume that there are ten separate volumes, each of which has a certain heft and density. Your brain will read the lines between the books as physical separations between the covers. But what if those lines were actually drawn on the surface of a "stack" that's actually a box designed to look like books but is secretly capacious enough to hide a rabbit or duck or bowl full of water? If the illusion is strong enough, this possibility would never even occur to you.

Keep this in mind the next time you see a magician make his assistant appear from a platform or table.

Here's another example. Let's say I want to steal a bunch of colorful silks from their hiding place behind a chair. First, I need to create a decoy reason for approaching the chair. So throughout the performance I'll habituate the audience to my use of the chair as a catch-all. Early in the show I'll toss my jacket onto it. Later I'll place a book on it. Gradually the audience is primed to assume that this is my designated discard spot. So when I set my wand on the chair and sneak my hand behind it to grab the silks, no one's the wiser. All *appears* perfectly ordinary, because I've *established* what is ordinary.

There is an important exception, however. Children, who are still figuring out which patterns are associated with which effects, are much less susceptible to priming. That's because kids make fewer assumptions and notice more of the details that adults skate past. So it's harder to suck them into my pattern habituation tractor beam. Often, for instance, I'll change one playing card into another with a wave of my hand. Adults are almost always stumped. If pressed, they'll come up with all sorts of inventive explanations, guessing that I'm using a digital card or color-changing ink—they'll even pick up the card and rub it between their fingers to see if the ink rubs off. But if there are kids in the audience, at least one is bound to shout out, "You had a second card behind the first!"

Children also are generally more open to randomness in their daily lives, less bound by routine and set expectations. Try walking through a park with a child, and you'll likely be surprised how much more the child notices than you do. Adults miss out on a lot, thanks to their own internalized priming. Just how much was demonstrated by two experiments that eliminated the audience habituation that typically precedes an artist's performance.

One of these tests was conducted in 2014 by the famously elusive street artist Banksy. He anonymously set up a stall in New York's Central Park and for one day sold his signed prints for $60 apiece. Bonham's auction house would value those prints at more than $75,000 each. Yet Banksy had only two buyers all day.

Like Banksy, renowned violinist Joshua Bell normally attracts high-paying audiences. His customary venues are concert halls. In 2007, however, he played for forty-five minutes for free in a subway station in Washington, DC. He wore street clothes and a baseball cap instead of his tux, but performed the same Bach pieces he would normally play onstage—and on a Stradivarius, no less! A hidden camera showed that of the 1,097 people who passed him, only seven stopped to listen.[7]

Without the usual priming patterns of context, publicity, and pricing, audiences were blind to the significance of Banksy and Bell, even with the artists right in front of them. Furthermore, most adults in the park and in the subway were so intent on their own routines that most would never have noticed them even if they did know who they were. Of the grand sum of $32.17 that Bell collected as tips, $20 came from the one and only person who recognized him. If only the others had had a child with them!

SUBTLETIES POWER SUGGESTION

In 2015, the Watson Design Group was tasked with creating a promotional campaign to generate buzz at Austin's South by Southwest (SXSW) media festival in advance of the premiere of the movie *Ex Machina*. The sci-fi thriller revolves around a young computer programmer tasked with determining whether a female humanoid named Ava can convince him that she's human.[8] In the film the Turing test administered to Ava is based on a real test, developed in the 1950s to see if a machine can pass for a human in online conversation. Since most of the festivalgoers were techies, they were an ideal audience both for the film's content and for a sneaky campaign to prime their interest in *Ex Machina*.

When I spoke to Watson strategist Arin Delaney about the project, she explained, "This was all happening around Elon Musk and Stephen Hawkings' public statements warning about the dangers of AI." It was also happening in the age of social media, when young single men like those at SXSW were wired into Tinder. So Watson used Tinder like a Trojan horse, to deliver Ava directly to unsuspecting festivalgoers. "We created a profile for Ava on Tinder to see if she could convince people she was human. We called it the 'Tinder Turing test.'"

Ava appeared on Tinder in a familiar pattern, as a twenty-five-year-old looking for dates. Her profile featured a photograph of the actress who played Ava in the film, and her responses to the more than four hundred Austin-based matches she received over her three days online were mostly computer generated, although the designers could add human responses, since blurring the boundaries between humans and robots was the whole point. Ava dropped a clue by asking every match, "What makes you human?" But most men were so enthralled by the illusion of this young beauty that they missed the point of "passing" her test as humans. Then Ava directed them to click the link to "my Instagram" . . . and they were taken to a photo and video promoting the film and inviting them to the premiere.

Some of Ava's matches felt stung by the deception, but they got over their disappointment fairly quickly when they realized the ingenuity of the tactics: The avatar had emotionally engaged every one of them before they even knew the movie existed! Most shared their experience aggressively on social media. The campaign received press coverage in *Time, Newsweek, Wired, Adweek,* and more than fifty other major news outlets. All this attention keyed up a debate over the ethics of presenting a bot as a human, but that conversation only drove more people to see the movie, which posted the highest-grossing opening weekend ever for its

⟶ EMPLOY THE FAMILIAR

distributor, A24. Made for just $15 million, the film went on to gross more than $36 million worldwide.

That's the power of suggestion.

To enhance this power, magicians often use "subtleties." If I were to have one envelope that I plan to switch for another, I might add a subtle tear in the envelope. Perhaps I point it out, perhaps I don't. But I do want the audience to see it, because when I switch it for the second one, the duplicate envelope also will have an identical tear in it. The audience sees this subtle pattern, and is convinced that it's the same envelope. But what's also working here is the illusion of choice—I allow the audience to arrive at this conclusion for themselves.

A subtlety, therefore, is something that we don't overtly state, but that, like Ava, we slyly encourage the audience to notice. It strengthens the illusion and gets people to jump to conclusions based on a small bit of evidence.

Subtleties are like patterns within patterns. One of the sneakiest examples in marketing today is the "native ad," which looks like editorial content online or in a newspaper, but is really promotion in disguise. You might think you're reading an article about different ways to build a skating rink in your backyard, but after you've read the article, which contains discreet images of the Canadian flag, Canadian beers, and the Toronto Maple Leafs' hockey emblem, you could well find yourself researching winter vacations in Canada. Nowhere in the "article" was Canada directly mentioned, nor was it identified as the source of information. No strongarming here. The connections are subtle, never overt.

Arin Delaney cites BuzzFeed as an online site that specializes in clever and compelling native ads. "The second list on the left side is ALWAYS an ad," she told me, "but most people can't tell." One reason is that it's given a position of importance. "It's a strategic placement, as it's 'above the fold' [you don't have to scroll to see it]." Another is that the content is interesting and entertaining, allowing readers to find their own unwitting but willing way to the target brand or product.

Subtleties can play a potent role in our choice to adopt new habits, as well as new products. For example: toothbrushing. Back in 1900, Americans brushed their teeth infrequently, and when they did they mostly used chalky tooth powders or dental pastes made with hydrogen peroxide and baking soda. Then an ad executive named Claude Hopkins began marketing Pepsodent. Within a decade, Americans of all ages were brushing their teeth morning and night in pursuit of a "Pepsodent smile." As Charles Duhigg writes in *The Power of Habit*, Hopkins achieved this feat initially by priming a widespread craving for beauty.

He planted the idea through ads that Pepsodent could deliver whiter, cleaner, prettier teeth. Then he reinforced this idea by drawing attention to the feel of dirty teeth, which he linked to looks and promised to change. "Just run your tongue across your teeth," one ad instructed. *"You'll feel a film*—that's what makes your teeth look 'off color' and invites decay."[9] Pepsodent would remove the film and—voilà!—beautiful teeth. Just like a magician, Hopkins habituated his audience to make a specific association between his cause and a desirable effect. But something else set Pepsodent apart from the many competing toothpastes that sprang up in the wake of Hopkins's hugely successful campaign. That something was a powerful subtlety.

Unlike the competitors, Pepsodent contained citric acid, as well as mint oil, and this recipe produced a distinctive aftereffect. When you brushed with Pepsodent your mouth tingled. That tingling sensation, along with the minty taste, signaled your brain that your teeth were clean and "beautiful." And pretty soon, that tingly sensation became part of the reward package that you came to expect, and then crave. If you forgot to brush, or used another toothpaste that didn't produce the tingle, your mouth wouldn't feel clean, and you wouldn't like it.

As Duhigg writes, "Claude Hopkins, it turns out, wasn't selling beautiful teeth. He was selling a sensation."[10] In other words, he was selling a subtlety that people weren't even aware they were craving.

Experimental psychologist Charles Spence studies just these sorts of subtleties at his Crossmodal Research Lab at Oxford University.[11] The connective tissue in his research consists of the pathways that integrate information from the five human senses to shape our perception of reality. He wants to understand how what we see or hear, for example, affects what we taste. His experiments identify basic subtleties that make one product more appealing or effective than its identical twin. For example:

- Coffee from a white cup tastes more intense but a third less sweet than coffee served in a glass mug.
- But a white container makes strawberry mousse taste 10 percent *sweeter* than a black container.
- If you listen to low-pitched music while eating bittersweet toffee, it will taste 10 percent more bitter than with no music.
- Salted popcorn tastes sweet if served in a red bowl.
- Cheesecake served on a round plate tastes 20 percent sweeter than the same cake served on a square one.
- Beer from the same glass will taste more, or less, bitter, depending on the background music.

The true cause of these effects likely has to do with pattern associations that have been encoded in the brain over millennia. Greens with angular leaves generally taste more bitter than round-leaved plants. High-pitched sounds and voices are associated in infancy with sweet mother's milk. Red fruit in the wild is more likely to be sweet, so our hunter-gatherer brains read redness as sweetness. These subtleties are so convincing that they make the illusion seem real.

It's not surprising that about three-fourths of Spence's research is funded by food and beverage companies and other industries. His findings are having a profound effect on the way companies are packaging and selling their products. Volvo, for instance, introduced headrest-mounted speakers in its 2015 FH trucks after Spence discovered that drivers look forward more quickly when sound comes from behind the head, rather than from the sides. And after he studied male and female responses to different types of aerosol sounds, Unilever repackaged its Axe deodorant to spray with a louder, more aggressive sound than the aerosol on its Dove brand.

Subtleties can also be used to address public health problems. Spence is working with a children's cancer center in Spain to find ways of serving or packaging food to counteract the metallic taste and nausea created by chemotherapy. Other possibilities include packaging food for people with hypertension in blue containers, which will make it taste saltier and reduce their actual salt consumption. Or attacking the obesity crisis by using red packaging to make food seem sweeter while reducing the actual amount of sugar consumed.

At Schiphol Airport in Amsterdam the authorities used a brilliant subtlety to solve a dirty problem:[12] Men were making a mess around the urinals in the bathrooms. Jos van Bedaf, manager of the cleaning department, suggested providing something to aim at, men being naturally fond of target practice. Better yet, the target should be something the men would want to get rid of. Like a housefly. So when the terminals were renovated, each urinal was inscribed with its own fly in the basin. By subtly encouraging a bathroom pissing contest, Schiphol succeeded in reducing spillage between 50 and 80 percent.

The common denominator for all these strategies is their ability to tweak expectations and behavior with minimal strong-arming. The audience is barely aware that their perceptions are being directed. They believe *they* are in command, and that makes them both cooperative and enthusiastic. As any illusionist will tell you, if you call attention to your subtlety, that will only detract from its effectiveness.

MENTAL JUDO

In 2005, Amy Webb was a thirty-year-old self-proclaimed "data nerd." She put her love for data to use when she founded Webbmedia group, a leading digital strategy firm whose annual Trend Report quickly became a must-read for insights on groundbreaking technology and developers "to watch." Webbmedia has since created digital and mobile strategies for Time Inc., American Express, and CNN. But despite her digital expertise, Webb had a far less golden touch when it came to online dating. After she went out with one man who mentioned he had a wife as if this were an inconsequential afterthought, she'd had enough. She wasn't done with online dating, but she was done letting computer algorithms determine her choices.

SPELLBOUND

Webb knew what success looked like: an online dating profile that connected her with a mate for life, or at least a selection of genuinely promising prospects to choose from. But how could she reduce the randomness and take control of the process? Though she didn't realize it, the strategy she came up with mirrored a magician's approach to reverse-engineering the audience's pattern expectations. I call this technique "mental judo" because, like judo, the idea is to leverage the opponent's weight in my favor—to create an illusion. Amy Webb would use mental judo to gain command of the men *she* desired.

She began by reviewing her original dating profile. She'd filled in the "about me" fields honestly, but without particular care or attention to detail. To potential matches, she would not stand out. More to the point, she hadn't given any thought to the patterns of characteristics that would appeal to the men she sought.

So Webb turned the tables. She created ten fake male accounts through which to research how other women were presenting themselves and to identify those who were getting the highest volume of male responses. Then she engaged ninety-six of these popular women in online conversations and charted in complete detail how their data (height, hobbies, jobs, favorite places to travel) were processed by the site's male users. Some of the patterns she identified among the most popular females:

They used an upbeat and optimistic tone of voice. The most common words they used were *fun*, *girl*, and *love*.

They showed more skin in their photos, and the pictures were flattering, rather than silly or professional.

Nonspecific language was more effective. For example, saying you like dramas cast a wider net than saying you like *The English Patient* (which might drive away someone who hates Ralph Fiennes).

⟶   **EMPLOY THE FAMILIAR**

The profiles of the popular women averaged 97 words—short, sweet, and a far cry from some people's 2,000–3,000 word write-ups.

Popular women averaged 23 hours between communications, compared to more eager users who might respond instantly.[13]

With these data patterns in mind, Webb created a "super profile" that was optimized for the online dating ecosystem. Instead of uploading selfies in jogging pants, she selected pictures in which she was wearing nice dresses and smiling. She slimmed down her profile from 2,000 words to 90, and sprinkled it with words like *fun*, *adventure*, and *hope to travel*. The idea was to keep her profile honest but also to leverage the patterns of male preference so that she had her pick of the litter.

Men flocked to Webb's profile. They thought they'd clicked on their dream girl. Moreover, because the familiar structure of the dating websites helped create a false sense of randomness, they believed this was all a happy accident. Then, when the men emailed her, she'd respond in the same voice that she used in her profile. This bolstered the illusion and kept her in control of the selection process.

One of the men who clicked on her profile was an optometrist named Brian. Even after meeting Webb in person, he didn't know that she'd gamed the system. But that hardly mattered. Her conjuring had yielded the right result. By the time she revealed the mechanics of her trick, the magic had already done its work. Far from debasing reality, the illusion actually enhanced it. Brian was impressed by her proactive savvy, and soon they were married and starting a family.

The two were always a match. The matchmaker just needed to use a little mental judo to bring them together.

SPELLBOUND

As with regular judo, the key in mental judo is to start, as Amy Webb did, by identifying the hidden patterns that *already* influence your audience's choices and behavior. Magicians know, for example, that when we ask someone to name a favorite card, men often name the king or jack of spades and women the queen, ace, or seven of hearts. So we always have these cards loaded up in various pockets. In this regard, Webb's approach was really no different; she was just operating in a different theater, with a different goal.

The same was true of the Chicago safety engineers, a few years back, who needed to come up with a trick to slow down drivers on a treacherous stretch of Lake Shore Drive. Motorists, perhaps distracted by the spectacular views of Lake Michigan and the city skyline, had a bad habit of speeding past the 25-mile-per-hour limit and crashing on the sharp curves.[14] So the engineers considered what patterns normally govern drivers' perception of speed and danger—even when their conscious attention is otherwise engaged. They took their cue from optical illusion, and found that white stripes painted across the road at intervals could make drivers feel as if they were moving faster or slower, depending on the distance between the stripes. The less space between the white lines, the faster drivers feel they are going. And the *feeling* of exaggerated speed, the engineers reasoned, would be much more effective than any sign in warning drivers to slow down. So along the stretch leading up to the dangerous curves, a series of white lines were painted at intervals that got closer and closer. It worked because the painted pattern leverages the motorists' own instincts to change their behavior.

Facebook employs the same leverage less to change users' behavior than to keep them coming back for more. According to the *New York Times*, by several objective measures Facebook has grown into "the most powerful force in the news industry."[15] Many users freely admit that they get most of their news about the world from the streaming News Feed on their Facebook page, and CEO Mark Zuckerberg in 2016 had to host a personal powwow with political conservative leaders after they accused his social networking juggernaut of suppressing conservative viewpoints in its "Trending Topics" news section. Then the company came clean, sending shockwaves through traditional media, by admitting that its policy of news delivery is simply to give users what they want—even if the so-called news consists of baby pictures.

"Stories in News Feed are ranked," Facebook vice president Adam Mosseri posted, "so that people can see what they care about first, and don't miss important stuff from their friends. If the ranking is off, people don't engage, and leave dissatisfied." The value that drives this policy is connection, not information. "That's why if it's from your friends, it's in your feed, period."[16]

Give them what they want, especially if they don't realize it's what they want, and you own them. Mental judo.

Or, look at how music is employed by savvy commercial enterprises. In this case, the illusion works on the listener's sense of time. Slow music makes us feel as if we have more time, so we don't feel—or act—rushed. Studies have found that bars sell more drinks and grocery shoppers spend more than a third more time in stores when the background music is slow.[17]

Apple Stores alter customer time perception in a different way, by leveraging normal patterns of social engagement. A wait of ten minutes can seem like an eternity, or it can seem to pass quickly, and the difference can make or break customer satisfaction. In an ideal retail world, then, a salesperson would immediately rush to serve every customer who comes through the door. But Apple Stores are typically thronged with far more customers than there are trained sales specialists. What to do? Create an *illusion* that the customer's needs are being met quickly. Apple does this by using support staff to "reset" customers' internal clocks.

Apple trains its store greeters to immediately acknowledge every person who comes in, taking down their name and assigning them to a specific specialist with an estimated (and preferably realistic and reasonable) wait time. Just a couple of minutes later, another employee will touch base with the customer, confirming the name of the specialist. This contact resets the customer's sense of time. A couple of minutes later, the first greeter checks back with the information that the specialist is nearly ready, and that resets the clock again. With each contact, minor questions can be answered so the customer never feels ignored or forgotten. As long as the specialist really does turn up as soon as possible and provides attentive service, this strategy can significantly reduce customer impatience and enhance satisfaction.

Subtler forms of mental judo flip the meanings or triggers associated with patterns. In 2015 a "Museum of Feelings" popped up in Manhattan's Battery Park City. This free walk-through experience, patterned like a museum, allowed visitors by the thousands to have a multisensory adventure, passing through five kaleidoscopic rooms filled with constantly changing visual, tactile, auditory, and olfactory patterns designed to reflect joy, optimism, calm, invigoration, or exhilaration. The "museum" was thoroughly interactive. Its exterior changed color in response to social media data to "reflect New York's ever-changing mood." Inside, mirrors, fog, scent, and light patterns responded to visitors' movements and encouraged them to take selfies. Only when they reached the gift shop did they discover the whole experience had been sponsored by Glade—and the emotionally conducive scents were for sale under names like "Radiant Berries" and "Vanilla and Lavender."

Evan Schechtman, the creative director at Radical Media and who designed the project for Glade, based his concept on the fact that memory is intrinsically linked to emotion. Not only did this faux museum plant the idea that smell could help cheer people up or calm them down, but every visitor would leave with personal (presumably positive) memories associated with each featured scent. Those memories also would create an association between the Glade brand and this fun and novel "museum."

"I heard one couple walk into a room and say 'Wow, I didn't expect that at all,'" Schechtman told one reporter. "To me, that's mission accomplished."[18]

M usic videos provide a ready-made pattern for use in mental judo. One brilliant example is the video created by the Royal Canadian Mounted Police—Mounties, to you—in 2016. For six years the Mounties had been trying to get drivers to heed a law that required them to slow down and move to the farthest lane from any emergency vehicle with its lights flashing, but most Canadians still had no idea the law existed. As a result, Mounties were getting hit when they responded to roadway accidents. Then a group of Nova Scotia Mounties had an inspired idea while watching Toronto rapper Drake's "Hotline Bling" video. They would take the pattern of Drake's song and adapt his lyrics and moves to suit their own talents and purposes.

The resulting "Cop Light Bling" video features five Mounties wearing their Day-Glo yellow safety jackets, lip-syncing lyrics like

"Don't speed past my cruiser," and doing their own memorable version of Drake's drunk-uncle-at-a-wedding dance moves around a cop car with its lights blinking on a cold Canadian highway. The purposeful parody instantly went viral, attracted press coverage, and lit up the Twittersphere in Canada and beyond. Like a perfectly executed judo turnover, it caught the audience off guard, using their own preferences to get the better of them, and threw them for a loop. As one Facebook fan posted, "I did not know I had to go to the other lane. I am guilty of doing this before. Know better now."

And, she added, "Good way to communicate laws."[19]

Celebrities, of course, are a pattern unto themselves, and advertisers know that any product associated with celebrity will sell. Why? It's mental judo. Many, many consumers want to look, act, and feel like they, too, are famous, talented, and attractive. The power of association gives them the illusion that a little of that celebrity luster will rub off if they pattern themselves in the same jeans that Beyoncé wears, or the same model of car that Matthew McConaughey drives, or the same airline that Kobe Bryant flies—or even use the same dinnerware that Meryl Streep used to set the table in her last movie. Advertisers bank on this illusion, and are rarely disappointed.

Not all patterning is so sexy, yet even without the glitz and glamour, it works. Sometimes the only message it telegraphs is normalcy, and that's exactly what's called for. This was the marketing calculation that Chobani founder Hamdi Ulukaya made in 2007 when he introduced his yogurt to the American market.

His only significant competitor in the Greek yogurt sector at the time sold to specialty stores. Ulukaya was determined to take a different route. Even though the consistency, taste, and packaging of Chobani were different from the usual American yogurt brands, he wanted to send a clear message to shoppers that Chobani could fit right into the pattern of American yogurt consumption. Different, so to speak, but equal. And that meant getting it stocked in supermarket chains right alongside Dannon and Yoplait—*not* in the gourmet or natural food aisles.

"That's probably the single most important decision we made," Ulukaya later told the *Harvard Business Review*. "Within a couple of weeks after Chobani got into ShopRite, we started getting orders for 5,000 cases. The first time we received one, I kept double-checking to make sure it didn't say 500. It quickly became clear that our biggest challenge wasn't going to be selling enough yogurt—it was going to be making enough yogurt."[20]

They made enough, and Ulukaya's mental judo paid off. By 2016 Chobani was valued at $3 billion, with annual sales of more than $1 billion.

DEFY EXPECTATIONS: THE POWER OF DEVIATION

And yet . . . patterns, like rules, are made to be broken. And the moment to break them is when you want to galvanize *conscious* attention. If the power of mental judo lies in its leverage, the power of deviation lies in its boldness. The former is useful in slyly persuading others, the latter in blowing their minds.

This is what Arthur Koestler was getting at when he wrote in his 1964 tome, *The Act of Creation,* "Without the hard little bits of marble which are called 'facts' or 'data' one cannot compose a mosaic; what matters, however, are not so much the individual bits, but the successive patterns into which you arrange them, then break them up and rearrange them."[21] First find or make the pattern, then break it.

Koestler points to jokes as a prime example of this principle because the first two beats of every good joke create a pattern that misdirects the audience to form an expectation, which the third beat—the punch line—breaks. Here's a mordant example from Jon Stewart:

> I celebrated Thanksgiving in an old-fashioned way. I invited everyone in my neighborhood to my house, we had an enormous feast, and then I killed them and took their land.[22]

The first two beats in the series—inviting everyone and having an enormous feast—set up a cheery expectation, which the punch line turns on its head with a twist of surprise and meaning, as well as humor. Comedians describe this mechanism as the "rule of three."

What's important to remember is that the surprise must cast a new and memorable light on the pattern. Stewart's joke is effective because the ending changes the listener's interpretation of the beginning. So the three beats work together in a way that makes the final impression larger than the pattern that's been broken.

This mechanism works the same way in every area of innovation, whether in the arts, science, or business. The deviation that "works" is never arbitrary. It has to be strategic. Magic is no exception.

Most illusions have been around for ages, which means that creating brand-new ones is difficult. This is why magicians are always on the lookout for new technologies that can help them defy audience expectations. Robert-Houdin, with his use of the electromagnet to cow the Marabouts in Algeria, was following in the footsteps of Louis Döbler, who in 1842 was the first to use electricity in an illusion show. The German Döbler would fire a pistol at a row of two hundred candles. Behind the wick of each candle was a gas jet, connected by a conducting wire. Upon firing the gun, an electric current, a spark jumping from jet to jet, ignited each of the gas flames and thus each of the wicks. The underlying pattern was pure science, but to the audience who knew nothing of electricity, the whoosh of ignition was game-changing magic.

MIRACLES OF 1937

The classic illusion of sawing a person in half relies on the audience assuming that the figure lying onstage at the outset is a whole outstretched person. This assumption typically is reinforced at the end of the act, when the two "halves" are reunited and the figure rises. However, in 1937, the magician Rajah Raboid teamed up with Johnny Eck, the "Amazing Half Boy," to create an unforgettable deviation from the usual trick.

Eck had been born without a pelvis or legs. His body ended below the ribs, as if he were naturally halved. To most audiences, Johnny Eck was a living optical illusion. To Raboid, he was a gift. Advance notices for his "Miracles of 1937" show promised that he would "actually saw a man in half." Eck ensured that Raboid would deliver.

The magician conducted the trick by "sawing off" a set of fake legs from Eck's body. The spectators, of course, expected the trick to end in the usual way, with a whole man standing before them. Instead, Eck bounded off the table, walking on his arms and shouting, "I want my legs back." Meanwhile, the detached "legs" (oversize pants now occupied by a dwarf) started running around the stage with Eck chasing them.

The shock of seeing what appeared to be an actual halved man caused pandemonium to break out in the audience. Shrieking spectators would sprint for the exits—especially when Eck started chasing his legs up the aisles. But those who weren't irreparably traumatized by this pattern violation were awestruck. As they laughed and applauded, Eck was hoisted atop his legs and taken off-stage, to be replaced by his twin Robert, who strode out reassuringly whole. The pattern of normality restored, those left in the audience cheered.

The act became the toast of the East Coast and rewarded Raboid with packed theaters.

Identifying patterns that are ripe for the breaking is the essential first step toward deviation. Before Howard Schultz bought Starbucks in 1987, the company sold coffee beans only, out of six stores in Seattle. Most Americans at the time drank coffee they brewed at home or bought at the local diner. Coffee shops were an urban staple, but in all of the United States there were only about two hundred European-style coffeehouses that served espresso. During a trip to Italy in 1983, when he sipped his first latte, Schultz realized that America's coffee habit was a pattern he could profitably break by intersecting it with the Italian pattern. Four years later he bought out the original Starbucks owners and introduced the concept of the American chain coffee bar—Italian but with a Seattle twist of branding and polish.

Shaking up the old patterns was a huge and intentional part of the concept, as Starbucks then-CEO Orin Smith told *Fortune* in 2003. "We changed the way people live their lives, what they do when they get up in the morning, how they reward themselves, and where they meet."[23]

One measure of originality, Koestler wrote, is the extent to which "selective emphasis deviates from the conventional norm and establishes new standards of relevance." The operative words here are *selective* and *relevance*. In order to grab your audience's attention, you have to *selectively* change just the elements of the pattern that will make it—and you—more *relevant* to them.

Schultz made coffee taste different, but he also made it fit more conveniently and comfortably into the lives of customers who already drank coffee. Only after he'd won over this base did he go on, selectively tweaking his now-established pattern to make Starbucks relevant to customers who didn't even drink coffee. The artists Banksy and Bell did exactly the opposite when they presented themselves experimentally to unsuspecting and unprepared audiences in the park and subway. They were ignored in part because they made themselves *less* relevant than they would be in their normal contexts.

In 2011, the chain store Tesco tried an experiment that looks, on the surface, like a parallel to Banksy and Bell's: Tesco radically changed the environmental context for its stores in South Korea by turning subway platforms into virtual grocery stores. Unlike Banksy and Bell, however, Tesco's experiment broke the old pattern in a way that made it *more* relevant to the audience.

SPELLBOUND

Since many Korean commuters normally shop for groceries after work, Tesco figured they would already be primed to notice the life-size pictures of products and produce now lining the platforms. Once their attention was piqued, the deviation from the usual pattern would make them curious to find the posted directions, which explained that they could use their cell phones to scan the bar code beside any pictured item they wanted. If they did, their purchases would be delivered to their home that day. Tesco's online grocery sales rose 130 percent in three months, and registered users increased by 76 percent.[24]

That test inspired American grocery delivery service Peapod to try a similar campaign with more than one hundred virtual grocery displays in commuter rail stations throughout the United States. According to Peapod COO Mike Brennan, "When we piloted the virtual stores last fall, we found that the advertising stopped people—it engaged them, and we saw mobile app downloads as a result."[25] So the company took the next step, plastering their "market" on the sides of vans that would roam the way a Mister Softee truck would, making stops at parks, sports arenas, and other public gathering spaces. Only instead of buying a single ice-cream cone, customers could do their whole week's shopping without leaving the ballpark. The secret to success lay, as Koestler predicted, in breaking patterns in selective ways that made the new patterns more relevant than the old.

This is exactly what several brands are trying in retail stores, using virtual reality.[26] At Lowe's, customers can put on a headset, enter the "Holoroom," and see what their home renovation will actually look like with their purchases. This inverts the typical pattern of shopping for home improvements, which requires customers to guess what their purchases will look like after installation. By instead bringing the home virtually into the store, Lowes can give customers the illusion of guaranteed satisfaction.

At Toms Shoes' flagship stores, virtual reality alters the pattern of customer experience by making the intangible aspects of their purchase vividly visible. Toms is a proud "storydoing" company whose mission of global connection can provide customers with a strong incentive to choose Toms products over those of competitors. Toms tells customers that they can help change the world just buy purchasing Toms shoes, sunglasses, handbags, or clothing, in return for which the company will "provide shoes, sight, water, safe birth and bullying prevention services to people in need." But that connection could seem pretty remote for American families trying on shoes in a Toms store at the mall. Here's where VR headsets break the pattern. They allow shoppers *themselves* to virtually visit the foreign countries and children who benefit from their purchase of a Toms product. The illusion of being present in the schoolyard when Peruvian children receive their gift of shoes creates an experiential connection to help customers personally *feel* part of the global story that's so integral to the Toms brand. It heightens the associated narrative as well as the shopper's personal experience, and that benefits the bottom line.

When all the principles of illusion work together, the effect is irresistible.

CONJURE AN OUT

Back in the 1920s, the Great Blackstone was one of America's preeminent maestros of magic. His specialties included turning handkerchiefs into "dancing" spirits, making a lightbulb float, and plucking enough bouquets out of thin air to turn the entire stage into a blooming garden. With "the Phantom Stallion," he became famous for making a live horse disappear. But one night in Brooklyn, the horse failed to materialize at all.

That is, no one ever brought the horse to the theater. "Blackstone, the Master Magician" was already onstage performing his "Oriental Nights" revue. Ordinarily, he'd lead the horse into an open-fronted canvas tent, then close up the tent and, with the bang of a pistol shot, release the tent walls to reveal that the horse had vanished. In reality, the horse would be hidden behind a stage flat and then wheeled into the wings under cover of a scenery change. But without the horse first *appearing*, Blackstone could hardly impress anyone by making it disappear. So he stalled, performing smaller pieces and bantering with the audience. Still, no horse.

Blackstone needed what magicians call an "out." So he summoned his entire stage crew onstage and into the tent. Then, BANG!, he vanished his entire company.

But this was not the Great Blackstone's most legendary out. In 1942, he was performing a daytime show with a family audience at the Lincoln Theater in Decatur, Illinois, when he received a whispered message from his assistant. Blackstone glanced into the wings, then turned to the audience with a surprise announcement.

"Boys and girls," he said. "Today we are going to attempt something never before performed by a magician—a trick so large we can't do it inside the theatre."[1] Then he instructed everyone to exit in a particular order, six rows at a time, starting from the front. "When you're on the pavement," he instructed, "look up in the air." The children and their parents eagerly obeyed while the maestro watched to make sure no one violated his directions. Once they reached the street, however, the audience discovered to their amazement that the Great Blackstone's "illusion" was an actual fire blazing in the drugstore next door.

Those were real firemen extinguishing the flames, as it had been the real fire chief backstage furiously signaling the magician to kill his act. Instead, Blackstone used a masterful emergency out to prolong his show while also preventing what could have been a disastrous stampede of terrified families racing for the exits.[2]

THE ILLUSION OF SUCCESS

"Out" is a magician's term for a contingency plan or device that's deployed when a trick takes an unexpected turn and threatens to fail—or flat out *does* fail. Think of outs as insurance designed to protect the illusion of success.

Let me repeat that: Outs are designed to protect the *illusion* of success. The operative point here is that success without failure *is* an illusion, because failure plays so many vital roles in the creation of success. To name just one, in magic it's the tension between the prospect of failure and of success that keeps audiences interested and engaged, so a good illusionist needs *both* outcomes to seem equally imminent.

However, magicians, like masters of industry, thrive by keeping the importance of failure hidden—or disguised. We understand, accept, and generally exploit the fact that success is a confidence game, by which I mean that both performer and audience must maintain confidence in the performance at all times, *even as the palpable threat of failure escalates.* Onstage, this threat may appear in the form of a blade poised to slice a human in half; in industry it might present itself as a potential loss of millions on the balance sheet. Either way, success will ride on both the confidence and competence that the maestro commands. Magicians, like managers, who wield decisiveness, efficiency, and active know-how are generally the ones who reap praise and rewards.

But don't confuse confidence with arrogant claims of perfection. Confidence suggests readiness, a state of mind and skill that's both earned and assured, but for the full effect to succeed, it's always best to leave room for doubt—that vital gap between seeing and believing—on the audience's end. In my show, I always include a couple of incidents that I pretend to mess up, then get right, to reveal that I had things under control the whole time. That way nobody can tell whether I'm making a mistake for real, or as part of the act. This affords me more room to maneuver when something actually does go wrong, as it inevitably will.

The real benefit of failure is that it prepares us to succeed. Having blown plenty of tricks *offstage*, I know I can cobble together an onstage solution any time I need one. My confidence is no act. I've tested my skill set, my resources, my instincts enough to trust them, so I don't panic. Even when the solution hasn't been scripted, I never doubt my ability to find the best out, to turn any mishap to my advantage.

The ultimate power of outs, then, is that they allow us to retain our confidence while adapting quickly and effectively to unpredictable change. When moves fall flat, a device malfunctions, or some wise guy throws an unexpected challenge from the audience, outs allow us to retain command of the narrative and sustain the audience's belief in our abilities.

In his now-classic 1940 handbook *"Outs," Precautions and Challenges*, magician Charles H. Hopkins likened outs to military maneuvers: "In the science of warfare, strategy is the technique of selecting, holding, or changing a position. Quickest to reach fame are those whose strategy is always prepared for the worst. Surprised by an ambush and forced to retreat, they quickly reorganize and spring a surprise of their own. . . . As with war heroes, he rises to greatest fame whose strategy is capable of most skillful change in the face of sudden emergency."

We typically think of failure as a reversal of fortune, an unexpected obstacle, an attempt that misses its goal. But here's the critical thing to remember: Determinations of failure and success, like all illusions, lie in the eye of the beholder. What you see, think, and know are entirely different from your audience's perceptions.

A flub that you assume to be a failure may well go unnoticed by everyone else.

Vegas magician Mac King has a signature trick that requires him to load a live goldfish into his mouth seconds before he pulls it out and drops it into a glass of water held by an audience volunteer. But the first time he ever performed the trick onstage, he recalls, "that little fish decided to swim down my throat." King turned and threw up into a suitcase he kept onstage. The volunteer standing beside him "said 'Eeeeewww!' but no one else in the audience reacted." King had another goldfish, and his next try went according to plan. But that wasn't really an out; it shouldn't logically have erased the spectacle of his regurgitation from the audience's memory. Yet, after the performance, "No one asked me, 'Did you vomit onstage?' Everyone saw it. It's so weird. I don't know what's going on in people's minds."[3]

The lesson here: Don't assume, just because *you* know you've failed, that everyone else does. As the great Miles Davis once said, "If you hit a wrong note, it's the next note that you play that determines if it's good or bad." And that next note may be easier than you think. Both the eye and the ear of the beholder can be very forgiving—if unwittingly so.

FAIL . . . TO SUCCEED

Even when spectators do notice failure, it won't necessarily have the effect you fear. That fear, for most of us, involves extremely unpleasant doses of humiliation and blame, followed by their sorry twins, guilt and shame. But as Hopkins explains, "One very

⟶   CONJURE AN OUT

peculiar attribute of visible failure is that under certain conditions it may lead to greater success than otherwise."

For one thing, it makes us more sympathetic. Because audiences can't identify with perfection, they instinctively distrust performers who declare in advance that they "never fail." It's safe to say, however, that virtually every member of every audience has personally experienced failure and can empathize with uncertainty. This is why I never claim to be infallible. Instead, when I'm onstage I work to project courage, openness, and calm—optimism, but not cockiness. What I don't want is for them to bet *against* me and hope that I'll fail, which they will do reflexively if I claim to be perfect. What I *do* want is for them to be a little afraid for me, imagining themselves in my shoes.

As Hopkins observed, "Real or simulated perspiration only helps to build up the effect," which in turn creates an ideal launching pad for an out. "Remembering that the audience can only guess what you are going to do, an actual ready-planned method of escape puts you miles ahead of them. Final production of the selected card or naming it in some totally unexpected manner snatches victory from defeat and the customers will rave."[4]

The essential truth here is that, as Hopkins says, "[i]t is the 'switch' that does the trick." That switch, from failure to success, and the surprise and relief that go with it, turbocharge the audience's perception of triumph—as the success of the *seven* Rocky movies proves. Rocky Balboa is one tough fighter, and the audience hopes he's equal to champion Apollo Creed, but Rocky must valiantly lose (if only by a technicality) before the script will allow him to snatch victory from the jaws of defeat and finally knock his nemesis out. Though it's often said that everybody loves a winner, Rocky without failure would be a champion nobody could root for, much less pay money to watch.

SPELLBOUND

The point to remember is that failure of *process* does not have to spell *professional* failure. People don't mind seeing the wires now and then. Everyone makes mistakes. What really matters in the court of public opinion is winning *in the end*. That's because of a human tendency called survivor (or survivorship) bias.

This cognitive slant is summed up in the saying, "History belongs to the victors." Survivor bias creates the widespread assumption that only those who are ultimately successful "count." And this has real consequences. Children and adults alike turn naturally to winners as the source of all the lessons we really need to learn; losers are generally discounted, or ignored altogether. We do the same thing when we draw conclusions from the material, numbers, or witnesses that survive a process such as a mathematical calculation, scientific experiment, or criminal trial, and fail to factor in the evidence that was lost or discarded along the way. These conclusions are illusory.

As a magician, I take advantage of survivor bias all the time. Once, I was performing sleight of hand over drinks with a group of bankers the night before a show for their investment firm in Philadelphia. While chatting up one of the bankers, I touched the lapel of his blazer under the guise of complimenting his taste. "Nice material!" Meanwhile, under the cover of this larger action, I slipped the two of spades into his right jacket pocket. I wasn't quite sure what my plan was yet. If I'd had a duplicate two of spades, that would have been perfect, but I didn't, so I figured I'd do something with the two of clubs as the "mate" of the planted card. Before I could even fan the deck, however, another man challenged me. "If you're so good, why don't you just make a card appear? Like the two of spades."

Magicians can wait years for a gift like this. Don't screw it up, I thought. Don't rush it. If I were to reach straight for the jacket pocket, the trick would be "too perfect" and, therefore, suspect. Instead, I took steps to stretch and complicate the proceedings with theatrics. "Okay," I said to my challenger. "Two of . . . spades?" Let him think I was unprepared. I mimed taking an invisible card out of the deck, crumpling it in my hands, and moving it in the direction of my target banker's jacket. I came just close enough to his pocket to suggest that I was invisibly transferring the card, but not so close that an actual transfer was possible. Finally, I asked him to reach into his pocket himself . . . drumroll, please . . . and pull out . . . the two of spades!

People *flipped out*. Even my surly challenger, arms still crossed, muttered, "Not bad. Not bad," before tottering off.

Not bad! An effect this pure comes about only once every number of years, when coincidence collides with preparation.

But *that* is the magician's secret. Other people don't know what the end of the story or trick is supposed to be, so they can't differentiate between the utterly mind-blowing, 1-in-52, chance of getting the random card right, and the backup plan, which in this case, I never even needed to formulate. Instead, thanks to survivor bias, I was able to capitalize on sheer coincidence—as if I truly did have supernatural powers!

It's important to remember, however, that when the goal is not pure entertainment, survivor bias must be handled with care. Otherwise, it can lead to illusions that are both powerful and dangerous.

Consider the case of J. B. Rhine, a parapsychology researcher at Duke University in the 1930s who believed he'd found proof that some people have psychic abilities. Rhine's experiments involved a set of five Zener cards, which his colleague Karl Zener designed to test subjects for ESP. Each Zener card bore a simple symbol—a star, cross, circle, etc. Subjects were asked to state which card the examiner was looking at. What Rhine didn't realize was that the Zener deck is stacked by the laws of chance. Had he used a regular set of fifty-two playing cards, the probability of anyone guessing correctly would be low indeed, but with just five possibilities, the chances were excellent—especially if a subject was good at counting cards. Also, the larger the pool of subjects, the greater the odds that several would guess all the cards right.

Here's where survivor bias cooked Rhine's results. He *eliminated* everyone who chose the wrong answers, saying they were not "strong telepaths." Then he held up those who chanced to make it through all the qualifying rounds as "proof" that ESP exists. Leaving aside later evidence that Rhine's results may have been doctored, they have never been duplicated using methods that account for survivor bias.

Still, psychics build devoted clienteles by elevating their correct guesses about customers' marital states and deceased family members, while burying or disguising the wrong guesses. Most of us would call this fraud, yet millions of people around the world fall for the ploy, sometimes to the tune of thousands of dollars per session.

Survivor bias can be deadly, as well as expensive. During World War II this cognitive blindness nearly cost the Allies many more fighter pilots than ultimately did die during combat missions. That's because naval researchers initially concluded, after examining aircraft that had returned from bombing raids, that armor should be used to reinforce the wings, the fuselage, and the rear gunner—parts of the planes that had sustained the most damage.

A lone statistician named Abraham Wald took exception to this plan. He pointed out that survivor bias was leading the researchers astray. These planes had *survived* damage to the affected areas. That meant, Wald said, that the scars marked the areas where planes could *take* a hit and still make it back. Ideally, the Navy ought to study the planes that never made it back, but since that was impossible, the researchers needed to invert their interpretation of those bullet holes: The most important parts of the plane to armor were those that—by pure chance—had *not* been shot in the surviving aircraft. Wald's methods were used not only in World War II but also during the wars in Korea and Vietnam.

Still, we do not learn. In the scientific world survivor bias has created a widespread problem known as publication bias. Because successful clinical trials are so overvalued (especially when the research is funded by industry), unsuccessful trials often go unrecorded. Researchers at Stanford University in 2014 found that between 2002 and 2012 only one-fifth of sociological studies with negative outcomes had been published, and 65 percent had never even been written up. By contrast, 60 percent of studies with positive results were published. In a twist of irony, researchers in psychiatry and psychology (who might be expected to know better) were the most likely to publish only positive results.

Why does this matter? Because, as Abraham Wald showed, it's at least as important to figure out what *doesn't* work as what does. Later researchers will likely waste time and money repeating failed tests if there's no record of the failures. And let's say a major pharmaceutical company funds a slew of tests for a new cancer drug but only publishes the successful trials and buries the 80 percent that were neutral or failed. This creates the illusion that the drug is a grand success, when the totality of research actually shows it to be ineffective or even dangerous. In fact, only 40 percent of studies sponsored by industry ever appear in medical journals.[5] Want to take bets on whether these were the successful ones?

SPELLBOUND

Stockbrokers use the same method—burying their failures—to enhance their reputations as "winners." And so do some venture capitalists.

Investor Ron Conway has often been referred to as the "Godfather of Silicon Valley," but he could also be called the maestro of survivor bias. Since the early 1990s, Conway has invested in thousands of Internet companies. He's known for his personal touch, emails around the clock, and is meddlesome and pushy on behalf of his clients. "I couldn't care less who is mad at me as long as the entrepreneur comes out ahead," he says.

Ron Conway has been successful. Extremely. Groupon, Dropbox, Airbnb, to name a few—each has a valuation north of a billion dollars, and he reaped handsome returns as an early investor in "all" of these companies. What few people see, though, is how often Conway *fails.*

In reality, failure is built into his business plan through a strategy called "spray and pray" investing. He'll plant $50,000 to $200,000 of seed capital into scads of nascent start-ups—his current rate is an alarming one start-up per week. That's fifty-two a year. And to many of these companies, he's a savior. But about one-third of his investments are failures—complete losses to him. Another third break even. Only a third are bona fide successes, and only the rarest of them are megahits.

You could say it's all about spin. Conway is not required to feature AdBrite, eToys, Songbird, or any of his other losses on his resume, so he doesn't. Like any good magician, he knows that, when it comes to promoting success, what the audience *doesn't* see is as important as what they do.

At the same time, the Conways and Walds of the world are keenly aware that failure gets a bum rap. Even if the public never sees it, each loss is a treasure trove of vital information that can teach us necessary lessons and make us resilient. Uberinvestor Warren Buffett concurs. In 1991 he told his audience at the Emory Business School, "I've often felt there might be more to be gained by studying business failures than business successes. In my business, we try to study where people go astray and why things don't work."[6]

One reason failure is valuable is that it's so much more memorable than success. Praise and advancement are *desirable*, but screwing up, especially in public, is unforgettable. Managerial researchers Vinit Desai and Peter Madsen looked into the role of failure in aerospace firms, where the stakes are literally stratospheric. They reviewed more than 4,600 space launches and compared the track records of the 426 companies involved. "We found that the knowledge gained from success was often fleeting while knowledge from failure stuck around for years," Desai said.[7]

That's why many venture capitalists refuse to invest in a new enterprise if the founder has never undergone failure. There's a strong chance that this founder has no idea what he doesn't know, not to mention why he doesn't know it or how to figure it out.

All this means that, as creative technicians, we have to appreciate the value of failure, even as we orchestrate the *illusion* of success. This is the message that J. K. Rowling, surely one of the most successful authors of the century, delivered in her commencement address to Harvard's class of 2016.

The bottom line, Rowling said, is that it's "impossible to live without failing at something, unless you live so cautiously that you might as well not have lived at all—in which case, you fail by default."

SPELLBOUND

What most of Rowling's millions of fans don't know is that she herself, as a young woman, "failed on an epic scale. An exceptionally short-lived marriage had imploded, and I was jobless, a lone parent, and as poor as it is possible to be in modern Britain, without being homeless." And that led to her major awakening:

[F]ailure meant a stripping away of the inessential. I stopped pretending to myself that I was anything other than what I was, and began to direct all my energy into finishing the only work that mattered to me. Had I really succeeded at anything else, I might never have found the determination to succeed in the one arena I believed I truly belonged. I was set free, because my greatest fear had been realised, and I was still alive . . . rock bottom became the solid foundation on which I rebuilt my life.[8]

As Nietzsche said, "That which does not kill us makes us stronger." No one, with the possible exception of savants, opens with success. For the vast majority of us mortals it takes practice to make perfect, and failure in practice is unavoidable. Toddlers fall before they walk. Artists erase, blur, and rework first strokes as a natural part of the creative process. Writers, as Faulkner famously said, learn to "kill their darlings" in revision. Or, as Pulitzer Prize winner Richard Russo put it, "You write a book, and it takes you forever, and you make all kinds of mistakes, and then you finally figure out what you're doing. And you go back, and you take out all of the worst mistakes, the ones that you can find, and you make it look like you knew what you were doing all along. That's the final illusion."[9]

⟶   **CONJURE AN OUT**

Nobel Prize winners, too, conduct countless failed experiments for every triumphant discovery. Thomas Edison spun the necessity of failure this way: "I have not failed. I've just found 10,000 ways that won't work."

So, too, with magicians. I test out all my material, often hundreds of times, before I perform it publicly. But that last bit is key. I practice on friends and make my mistakes safely offstage—behind the curtain, so to speak—so that when I step out in a public arena, I can feel as confident as possible that I will succeed.

BUILD IN SAFETY OUTS

The magicians in the videos I used to watch as a kid taught me always to keep a box of small tricks in the wings offstage. That way, if the curtain malfunctions and doesn't go up, or one of my devices breaks, I can still treat the audience to magic, and they'll think it's part of the plan.

It is, in a sense. Contingency strategies and reserve tricks are what I call safety outs. Like a plan B, these outs enable us to take calculated risks and shoot for miraculous payoffs, but also to take a bow even if our preferred effect fails. As vital in business and personal life as they are in magic, they're invisibly woven into the structure of a performance—by design.

This means that the time to develop most of these outs is *before* launching a new endeavor, be it a product, enterprise, or relationship.

- First, instead of counting on every detail to go right, consider what's likely to go wrong. The curtain won't rise. It rains on your opening day. Your workers go on strike. Use your past failures to inform your safety outs.

- Now map out alternate routes to success, should your main road close. Be prepared to step in front of the curtain, take the opening indoors, keep your operation going with a skeleton crew while negotiating a compromise with the strikers. What would have saved you the last time, had you only planned for it?

- Assemble your own "box of small tricks," that is, all the equipment, reserves, and inside team members you'll need to implement your safety outs, if necessary.

- Finally, script your presentation to leave your options wide open, so you have leeway to use your outs, should you need them, *without alerting the audience.* The script should allow you to create the illusion that any deviations from the original plan are actually *part* of your original plan.

Safety outs take several forms, depending on whether the goal is to reduce the *risk* of failure, increase the *opportunities* for success, or do *both* simultaneously.

SAFETY OUT #1: THE BACKUP PLAN

Backup plans are designed to deploy only when some element of your optimal act misfires. They're not your first choice, but they'll save you from detectable failure. I learned about this type of out as a teenager watching demonstrations of easy-to-do tricks at magic shops.

In one classic trick the "psychic" declared, "I have made a prediction!" He'd place three poker chips on the counter—one green,

one red, and one white. Then he'd gesture to me and boast, "I know which color you will select!" Next he held up a piece of paper and a pen. "Think of any poker chip and this"—he tapped the pen against the paper—"will represent your choice. Please write down 'red,' 'green,' or 'white.'"

Let's say I wrote down "red." "You have committed your choice in writing. You cannot change it!" the magician would declare. "And I *knew* you were going to choose the red poker chip, which is why in a moment we will turn it over to find something written on the back." He continued, "But first, turn over the white one to make sure that nothing is written on it." I'd flip over the white poker chip. Nothing. "And please turn over the green one to show that there's nothing there as well." As predicted, nothing. "Now for the moment of truth . . . turn over the red poker chip, your choice." I turned over the chip to find, written on the back, "YOU WILL CHOOSE THIS POKER CHIP." The so-called psychic had hit the jackpot. Thanks to my selection, his plan A worked.

But what if I'd chosen white or green? He had no fear of that, because, though only one chip had writing on the back, he had a plan B and plan C in reserve. What's more, he'd scripted the trick to provide for these safety outs. Had the magician said, "Your choice will be written on the underside of the chip," that would have boxed him into just one ending of the narrative. Instead, he broadly declared, "I have made a prediction," which left him plenty of room. Remember, after the magician instructed me to think of a color, he'd said, "*This* will represent your choice," and tapped pen to paper. With that gesture, he created two more possible end-points: the pen, and the white paper.

If I'd chosen green, the magician would joke that "this" referred to the pen, because he'd inscribed on the side of the pen, "Your choice is green." If I'd picked white, he'd have me flip the paper over to reveal, written on the back in big bold letters: "YOU WILL CHOOSE WHITE." Thus, if I hadn't known the secret behind the trick, any of the three "proofs" would have convinced me that the magic shop proprietor had made a correct prediction. Then survivor bias would have nudged me to believe he actually had ESP.

Backup plans work much the same way in business, as demonstrated by Amazon's early design. When Jeff Bezos launched his online bookstore in 1995, Amazon's model was "sell all, carry few." The company physically stocked only about two thousand books, but offered more than a million. What could go wrong?

The whole plan depended on safety outs in the form of so-called drop-shipping partnerships with book wholesalers and publishers. If a customer ordered a book that Amazon didn't have in stock, the order would be forwarded to a safety out that did. And the illusion of Amazon's omnipotence was protected by the packaging materials and labels in which every book, regardless of actual shipper, was delivered. The customer receiving the book would see only that it had come "from Amazon."

The success of this system of backup shippers, of course, paved the way for Amazon to reverse course later, building massive warehouses of its own, drastically expanding its product offerings, and stocking almost everything it sold. Efficiency and delivery speed became the company's hallmarks, and then in 2006 came the big twist, with Fulfillment by Amazon.

All of a sudden Amazon *became* the backup delivery plan for smaller retailers just as it had once (secretly) been. Independent sellers now could rely on Amazon to ship orders that they themselves could not fulfill. The Amazon safety out had come full circle, from fallback to main attraction.

CONJURE AN OUT

A variation of the backup plan is the exit strategy that allows us to take a flyer on Something Big without risking total loss. In business, exit strategies are especially important when courting investors, who naturally want assurance that they'll profit in the long run, no matter what happens to the company. Even the most dazzling ideas or products can fizzle over time, or get overrun by competitors. And not every organization has the resources or capacity to sustain an innovation indefinitely. So safety outs should be built into the model from the get-go.

This was the thinking of entrepreneur Robert R. Taylor in 1980 when he branded a liquid soap in a distinctive pump dispenser as Softsoap. Knowing that his product would be swamped by imitations, Taylor bought out all the pump dispensers in manufacturers' inventory. This secured a full year's head start and helped make Softsoap a unique hit, with sales of more than $25 million in the first six months and $100 million in year two. But Taylor knew that his relatively small company, the Minnetonka Corporation, couldn't protect the brand long-term, so he had his escape route ready: He'd sell the brand to a larger firm as soon as sales showed the first sign of turning. That took seven years. Then Minnetonka sold Softsoap to the behemoth Colgate-Palmolive, and Taylor went on, relying on the same exit strategy, to develop the first pump anti-plaque toothpaste, as well as the mega-perfumes Obsession and Eternity. Finally, in 1989, Taylor pulled his ultimate parachute. He sold Minnetonka itself to Unilever for $376 million.[10] [11]

Another type of exit strategy is insurance. Obvious as this may sound, the benefits of insurance as an out should not be underestimated. When the furniture innovator IKEA's flagship store in Stockholm, Sweden, burned nearly to the ground in 1971, insurance provided founder Ingvar Kamprad with the funding not just to rebuild but also to test a new approach to organization that included self-service. This new system radically increased IKEA's customer capacity while decreasing costs. Kamprad snatched victory from the jaws of defeat, but it was only possible because he invested in his ho-hum safety out in advance.

A third type of backup plan is a variation on a practice that performers call "stooging"—when secret confederates are planted in the audience. Television shows with live audiences, such as *Saturday Night Live*, often use not-so-secret stooges who are actually cast members. When magicians use stooges they're also part of the planned act; they're in on the methods behind the illusion and are there to fool the audience. So, technically, stooges in this context don't function as outs.

Also, stooging in magic is controversial. In the seminal *Expert Card Technique*, coauthors Jean Hugard and Frederick Braue write that the magician who uses confederates "is accepting the applause of his audience under false pretences [*sic*]; he does not merit their approval, since he has done nothing, and he knows it." Nevertheless, many magicians, especially those who perform on network television, hold that there's nothing wrong with using stooges if it guarantees the entertainment of millions of people.

Likewise, secret confederates can be used as valuable backup insurance in other contexts. Max Bazerman, a Harvard Business School professor, told me that, for him, an out is most needed "when a student says something irrelevant or inappropriate and you really do not know what to say next, or do not want to be on record responding to it." If Bazerman were to reveal that he was stumped, he'd risk losing control of his class. So instead he'll enlist the rest of his audience as his out by asking, "What do other members of the class have to say to that comment?" Better yet, he'll turn to students he can trust to come up with appropriately pithy, thoughtful, or intriguing remarks that will get the discussion back on track.

Similarly, in an interview there's no better way to maintain absolute control of the circumstances than by supplying the reporter with a list of questions that you're already prepared to answer. This serves as a safety out for both the interviewer and interviewee, ensuring that the interview goes smoothly and preventing any awkward silences—especially valuable if you're doing a live interview on-air or before an audience.

Robert B. Cialdini, author of *Influence at Work*, gives this same advice to scientists, who frequently find themselves in interviews with reporters who are not well versed enough in the topic to frame an accurate question. When good questions are provided ahead of time, Cialdini says, "[e]veryone wins. The media people get to inform and intrigue the audience with developments from the world of science, and the researcher gets to focus on those aspects of the work that he or she views as having the greatest import and scientific grounding."[12]

A TRICK WITH NO OUT

Sometimes the hazards of a trick defy the power of any out to override them. One such act is called "Russian roulette."

Also known as "nail roulette" or "Spike," the dangerous stunt challenges the magician to know which of several mixed-up paper bags contains an upward-pointing nail. Using his "sixth sense," the performer discerns which paper bags are "safe" and slams his hand down on the bags to prove there is no nail.

Occasionally the magician gets confused about where the spike is, and smashes his palm onto the nail. As you can imagine, this error ends the show, as the magician runs howling from the stage.

In an even more dramatic variant, a performer might coax an audience participant to test a bag that the magician has deemed safe. This, too, has gone terribly wrong. One Polish conjurer, on live television in June 2016, persuaded the host of the show to trust him—and she wound up impaling her hand.

When performing a dangerous illusion, the importance of outs cannot be overstated. If no out can be conjured to prevent or escape injury, then the trick may not be worth the risk. This was the calculation of the Magic Castle, which banned the performance of Russian roulette in 2015.

SAFETY OUT #2: STACKED DECKS AND HEDGES

While backup plans serve to prevent failure, stacked decks give a magician extra chances for success. They optimize the upside.

Let's say that I offer to make four face cards appear. "Would you like jacks, queens, or kings?" I ask. "Free choice." But the deck is already stacked in my favor. For easy access, I've placed the four kings on the bottom and the four queens on top. From those two

CONJURE AN OUT

locations I can easily make them appear in a magical way. And the jacks, chosen slightly less than the other two, are all together in the middle of the deck. But I know I can cut to them easily, probably without you even noticing the move.

Or, imagine this basic trick, in which I physically stack the deck so that it consists of just four cards: the six of spades, the king of clubs, the nine of hearts, and the ace of diamonds. The variety of colors and patterns in the deck now affords me the opportunity to fan them faceup to the audience. To one looking quickly—and that's everyone in the audience—the deck looks fair. If I then have a volunteer pull any card, look at it, and remember it, all I have to do is ask a couple of questions to narrow the possibilities to one. "Is it a red card?" "No? . . . ah, so it's a black card!" (All misses become jokes.) "Is it a face card?" "Yes? Ah, so you are thinking . . . of . . . the king of clubs."

Smart investors take a similar approach when building their portfolios. Consider Ron Conway, the aforementioned king of "spray and pray" investing. It might look as if he's just throwing money at random start-ups to see which ones hit, but he actually hedges his risk by conducting intense due diligence on each prospect before committing a penny to it. He only takes pitches that come through referrals, and for every company that his firm SV Angel bankrolls, another twenty-nine get rejected. In other words, Conway never gambles blindly.

Nor do other successful entrepreneurs. As sociologist Michel Villette and historian Catherine Vuillermot wrote in their 2009 study of business heroes, *From Predators to Icons*, "Risk taking is not very helpful in describing major success in business." It's more accurate to say that risk *reduction* is a requirement for success. The icons in this sample, who included billionaire business magnates

Warren Buffett, Bernard Arnault, Jim Clark, and Sir Richard Branson, "often outlasted their competitors because they were able to arrange localized and temporary procedures that made them less exposed than their direct competitors to the vagaries of the marketplace."[13] It cost Arnault 40 million francs to take over the flailing Boussac textile company, but Boussac included Christian Dior and Le Bon Marché department store. The immediate resale value, with assets like those, was many times more than Arnault's cost, so where was his risk?

The icons also included French aviation pioneer Marcel Dassault, who, as part of a performance study of aircraft for the French Army, recommended a new design for the planes' propellers in 1916. He then converted a furniture factory into a propeller manufacturer. Within a year, Dassault was building whole aircraft, for which he insisted the military pay him in full, in advance. This is called hedging your bets.

Especially in an era of what former Federal Reserve chairman Alan Greenspan dubbed "irrational exuberance," risk-hedging requires the ability to see *through* illusion. Nobody proved this more acutely than investment manager John Paulson, who traded *against* the housing bubble when most of Wall Street was doubling down on it. Paulson's stacking of the deck consisted of scrupulously analyzing the data and *not* believing in marketplace "magic" that defied the fundamental laws of economics. Before he made his bet he knew the odds as well as I do when I ask someone to pick a favorite card. Paulson concluded that the entire mortgage industry would implode the minute housing prices stopped climbing—and they were overdue to fall. So he bought insurance against millions of dollars of mortgages, using the now-infamous instrument called the credit default swap. When the bubble did burst, in 2007 and

⎯⎯⎯⎯→   **CONJURE AN OUT**

2008, Paulson's out *made* $20 billion for his company, while the rest of the world lost an estimated $15 trillion.[14]

SAFETY OUT #3: JAZZ, OR MIDSTREAM ITERATION

I often compare a seasoned card worker to a jazz musician. In fact, we magicians call it "jazz" when we manipulate a chosen card or cards throughout the pack without any prescribed plot to the trick. We know so many moves that we're confident we can shift and combine them at will. Our outs aren't planned, but we know they're there. And as always, because we haven't told anyone what the end of the story is, we can choose the path that best serves us.

Often, I'll start by showing the audience the ace of spades, then produce it again and again using a variety of unscripted shuffles and cuts. These moves are a magician's equivalent to a guitarist's chord progressions. We practice them until we can perform them without thinking.

Jazz can also involve the kind of opportunism that served me with those bankers in Philadelphia. If I happen to notice that a spectator's purse is open, there are moves for "put-pocketing" a card so that it "magically" appears in the purse at the finale of the trick. If I see that someone has set a drink down, I can use misdirection to slide a card underneath the glass and then invite its discovery. Jazz means improvising, to create an illusion at any given moment.

Because of the combination of tried-and-true methods with immediately available opportunities, jazz simultaneously reduces risk *and* increases the chances for success. In business, today's term for this kind of shapeshifting is "iteration." It happens mid-stream, in process, with little advance warning, like the inexplicable changes on your Facebook page. As CNET News writer Caroline McCarthy explains this process, "Old products are killed. New ones are rolled out one at a time, rather than bundled together in a huge annual relaunch. Experimental features emerge and disappear."[15]

Iteration is like on-the-job training. It happens out in front of the audience, but under close supervision. So the stakes are real, yet low. If a trial works well, it will be advanced to the next iteration. If not, the next attempt will be tweaked to prevent what went wrong. The sum of the input should increase accuracy with each incremental round. Meanwhile, the great wheel of the overall operation keeps on turning—with iteration, but without interruption.

The Japanese version of this is *kaizen*, or "continuous improvement." Toyota put *kaizen* at the center of the Toyota Production System, which dates back to the aftermath of World War II. "The goal is not to make huge, sudden leaps but, rather, to make things better on a daily basis," explained business writer James Surowiecki in a 2008 article about Toyota for the *New Yorker*. "Instead of trying to throw long touchdown passes, as it were, Toyota moves down the field by means of short and steady gains."[16] Most of the gains involve small changes, such as a redesigned signal cord or card system, or a reorganization of parts on a shelf. Not every idea works. "But cumulatively, every day, Toyota knows a little more, and does things a little better, than it did the day before."

One of the basic assumptions behind iteration is that nothing remains the same. Conditions and costs change. Workers change. Customers and their needs and desires change. Constantly. To survive, an organization has to be nimble enough to respond to these changes. That's what makes iteration an out. It trains an organization to keep options open, constantly scan for new opportunities, and learn how to adapt. Like illusionists, companies that iterate both underpromise and overdeliver.

———————→ **CONJURE AN OUT**

The result can look like magic, as UPS found after a manager posed the novel question, "Can we cut fuel costs by avoiding left turns?" UPS has a policy of encouraging experimentation, as long as it "never touches the customer."[17] This means, in effect, that nobody directly messes with the processing of packages, but all other systems are open for iteration. So instead of shutting this manager down, his bosses encouraged him to try out new routing strategies that directed UPS delivery trucks to navigate away from left turns and use right turns instead, thus cutting down on mileage and idling time. This single change saved 8.4 million gallons of fuel a year.[18]

THE EMERGENCY OUT, WHEN YOU'VE "SHOT THE WORKS"

Good old Charles Hopkins was pretty blunt when it came to failing publicly. "When you have 'shot the works' the fiasco is out in the open," he wrote. "If a forced momentary retreat or set-back becomes evident to the audience, an immediate change of strategy must be made." This strategy, which I call the emergency out, takes control of the unplanned situation and quickly turns it in a new direction. "The audience does not know it, but they have seen the end of one trick and are about to witness the beginning of another." Like an aerialist's net, the emergency out protects your survival even if there's no way to save the immediate act.

You'd think this lesson would be second nature to the all-time most famous illusionists, but even the greats sometimes are unprepared for the worst-case scenario. If you ask magicians about the biggest magic disaster ever, it's hands-down Harry Blackstone Jr.'s performance at the 1987 Orange Bowl halftime show—on live television. Blackstone Jr. was the son of the Great Blackstone, so he literally had magic in his blood. He should have had an out for every occasion, as his father did. But this TV performance had been bedeviled by windy conditions. Everything that could go wrong had gone wrong. Now he was supposed to materialize the Orange Bowl Queen out of an empty chamber for his grand finale. As he gestured dramatically at the box, the whole audience, live and at home watching on television, could see that she was stuck in the secret lift bringing her up from below stage. Her sparkly cape had snagged in the elevator, jamming it between "floors." It didn't help that the smoke machine, which was supposed to cover the whole process, also failed. Worst of all, Blackstone had no out. He'd lost control of his narrative.

This fiasco became an alert to everyone in our business: *Always* be prepared to conjure an emergency out.

There are so many factors that contribute to failure, above and beyond the performer's ability. Sometimes circumstances are simply beyond our control—and impossible to plan for in advance. Then what? Emergency outs are not about avoiding disaster. They're about rebounding from it.

The most common reaction to an unforeseen problem or mistake is to scramble to fix or excuse the situation. Most of us have emergency outs that we implement without thinking: pleading for sympathy to get out of a speeding ticket; turning a graceless stumble into a dance move; showing up with a favorite dessert to make up for arriving late for dinner. Misdirection is a standard component of emergency outs, as we try to get the audience to pay attention to something other than our error.

CONJURE AN OUT

DEATH OF A ROYAL CHINESE CONJURER

During the Golden Age of Magic, the theaters and music halls were bursting with colorful characters. My favorite of these showmen was Chung Ling Soo (1861–1918), the self-proclaimed court conjurer to the empress dowager of China. Soo rose to prominence in the 1900s, touring the globe with his majestic stage show and, alongside Houdini, becoming one of the highest-paid entertainers on the vaudeville circuit. Despite engineering some of magic's most hallowed illusions, however, Soo is best remembered for the fatal consequences of his failure to have an emergency out.

On March 23, 1918, at the Wood Green Empire theater in London, he was performing his famous bullet-catch feat, which he dubbed "Condemned to Death by the Boxers." But as the shots rang out this night, instead of plucking the bullets out of the air and dropping them on a porcelain plate, Soo clutched his chest and staggered toward the wings. This was not part of his act.

For his entire career Soo had never spoken a single word onstage. Now he gasped in perfect English, "Oh my God. Something's happened. Lower the curtain." He was rushed to the hospital, but by early morning the great conjurer was dead.

Soo would have had to be truly clairvoyant to have come up with an out for the circumstances that killed him. An inquest of the rifles revealed the following: The bullet was never meant to fire. Instead, a blank charge was fired from the ramrod tube. But grains of fine gunpowder had seeped through the well-worn threads on the breech plug, forming a fuse in the upper barrel. On that fateful night, enough gunpowder had amassed to fire the bullet as well as the blank.

Shortly after Soo's death, the public learned a shocking secret. The magician was really an American named William Robinson, a brilliant stage engineer who had worked with the illustrious illusionists Harry Kellar and Herrmann the Great. At the time, Oriental impersonation in magic shows was enormously popular because it simultaneously enhanced the mysticism of illusion and mocked the Chinese. Robinson had capitalized on this craze and parlayed it into a whole career.

Robinson's final words were the only ones, during the lifetime of "Chung Ling Soo," that he ever spoke publicly in English. When interviewed, he would speak mock-Chinese gibberish to a "translator" who converted his comments into English. His wife, Dot, masqueraded as Suee Seen, his doting Oriental bride. And for backstage interviews, Robinson always wore his hair in a queue, was enrobed in Chinese silk, and had black paste applied to his teeth. According to the *Weekly Reporter* in 1905, "His skin is yellow, his eyes are black and oblique, and his teeth are absolutely inky as those of all true celestials of rank should be."[19]

Though it had been suspected from time to time that Soo was actually an American, the public was wholly taken with this character. As one of Robinson's contemporaries, English magician Will Goldston, put it, "Chung Ling Soo has succeeded, because he has always presented to the public that which they like and not which he might prefer."[20] He succeeded, that is, until his lack of a final out "outed" him.

EMERGENCY MISDIRECTION

Of course, Blackstone Jr. notwithstanding, most magicians are such masters of misdirection that their emergency outs are almost undetectable. Indeed, audiences rarely have any idea how often stage illusions fail completely. Back in the 1930s, for instance, the magician Fred Keating was famous for making a canary cage disappear—bird and all. But one night, just as he was about to perform the trick, Keating realized that something was wrong: "I glanced suspiciously at the cage that was handed me, for I could tell from the 'feel' that it was not my old friend. The bird was the same, but I could sense that the cage had been tampered with. I could feel a horrible thumping in my heart."[21] In fact, someone had broken into his trunk and forced open the top drawer to get a better look at the cage. But as he was standing there onstage, Keating didn't know whether the device would work or not.

So, just as Blackstone Sr. had when his horse failed to show up, Keating announced that he was going to treat his audience to something new. He then made the bird alone disappear *out* of the cage. The crowd was thrilled, as they should have been—they were in the hands of a master illusionist who never lost control of his narrative.

Success, then, depends not just on hiding missteps but, better yet, using them to strengthen the illusion of command going forward, to leverage failure into victory and make the audience cheer in the process. By turning each failure into an act of redemption, you create the illusion that you are in command for the long haul.

Few examples prove the value of misdirection in times of crisis better than Winston Churchill. After the fall of France to Germany in May 1940, the British government withdrew its Expeditionary Force and British citizens were in a state of shock and panic. The Battle of Britain was about to begin, and the Allied defeat in the

Battle of France seemed a grim portent of the future. But in June, the brand-new prime minister staked his leadership on emergency misdirection. Churchill stepped repeatedly to the microphone and broadcast what can only be described as a motivating illusion to radios in every home in the United Kingdom. Instead of allowing citizens to look back at the recent disaster, he focused them first on a battle cry of strength, defiance, and determination: "We shall fight on the beaches, we shall fight on the landing grounds, we shall fight in the fields and in the streets, we shall fight in the hills; we shall never surrender."

Churchill cast Hitler not as a victorious foe, but as a kind of mythical beast, a "sinister" perversion, and instead of acknowledging the fractious political infighting that had hobbled Britain's earlier efforts against this menace, he emphasized the long and noble "continuity of our institutions and our Empire."

Finally, to direct his listeners away from terror and despair, Churchill appealed to British solidarity and strength that "Europe may be free and the life of the world may move forward into broad, sunlit uplands." To stoke his country's pride, he predicted that, a thousand years on, British "men will still say, This was their finest hour."

It can't have been easy, but it worked. These speeches galvanized the British people to unite against Hitler and rally around Churchill's leadership.

Emergency misdirection defies expectations. In the face of catastrophe, it trains the audience's attention on the upside, even if that upside has yet to be generated. Churchill proved this possible. So did a factory owner named Aaron Feuerstein after his Massachusetts mill burned down in 1995.

The mill that Feuerstein's family had owned for ninety years was in ruins, and 3,200 people stood to lose their jobs: downside.

And they wouldn't easily be able to replace those jobs, since factories were closing and corporations laying off workers throughout New England: downside. Feuerstein was seventy, old enough to take this disaster as a sign that it was time to close the factory for good: downside. But although thirty-three workers had been injured in the blaze, no one was killed: upside.

Although the mill was scheduled to expand, none of the already purchased state-of-the-art equipment had been touched by the fire: upside. And Feuerstein had always been generous with his workers, paying them more than other mill owners and providing full benefits: upside. He was Jewish, Orthodox, and had a profound sense of moral responsibility: upside.

Three days after the fire, Feuerstein stood before his audience of workers and announced that he would rebuild the factory . . . and keep them on his payroll for at least another couple of months. His audience applauded, and wept, with relief and gratitude.

This emergency misdirection captured the attention of the entire country. After the story hit the nightly news, Feuerstein received thousands of letters of praise and encouragement, along with hundreds of thousands of dollars in donations to help support his workers. President Clinton invited him to the State of the Union address. Three years later, Feuerstein was awarded the Courage of Conscience Award from the Peace Abbey Foundation, placing him in the company of the Dalai Lama, Mother Teresa, Rosa Parks, and Muhammad Ali.

DIRECTIONAL PIVOTS

When I was twenty-four, I quit my job and moved to Hong Kong for two years. I'd never gotten to know the Chinese half of my extended family while growing up, so, in theory, the reason I made this move was to explore my heritage. In reality, I tutored kids, hung out with magicians, went to jazz clubs, and ate a lot of dumplings. I enjoyed myself, but career-wise it was what you'd call a detour, a two-year hole in my resume with nothing to show for it but an exotic address. Near the end of those two years, I started thinking about the job applications I'd face when I got back to the States. How was I going to justify all this time abroad? I needed an emergency out, and fast.

Now, there's a closely guarded illusion in Chinese magic called *bian lian*, which literally means "face-changing." This seemed an apt metaphor for what I needed to do. The trick dates back to the eighteenth century and enables performers wearing painted masks to transform themselves in an instant with the flick of a fan or cape—a movement so fluid that you never see the old face disappear. Less than a month before my scheduled flight home, I decided to travel to Chengdu, in the Szechuan region, to "study" this ancient practice.

First, I needed an opera master who would be willing to teach me the trick on short notice. This was no easy task, since it meant he must also be willing to disclose a method that's generally passed down only from father to son. I called on my connections, called in favors, and finally I found a master who agreed. But he made me swear never to name him, as he was breaking his code of secrecy.

I spent my last two weeks in China struggling to follow the master's routine and learned only the first rudimentary moves. Back home my *bian lian* props would hang useless in my closet, a proper reminder of the true work required to master the illusion of face-changing. Nonetheless, I announced on my resume that I'd spent the two years in China "connecting with my heritage and

CONJURE AN OUT

searching for the closely guarded secrets behind the ancient art of *bian lian*."

That trip to Chengdu gave credibility to a two-year sojourn that might otherwise have given prospective employers pause. What I'd executed was a pivot, an abrupt shift of direction to get out of a downward spiral, to snatch victory back from (self-inflicted) defeat.

Politicians pivot all the time. In debates, they'll often deflect unwanted questions by using a technicality to return to a previous question, or else deliver a prepared position on an entirely different issue. In interviews, they sometimes seem to go conveniently deaf, ignoring the question altogether as they spin to a new topic. Whether the pivot is used to dodge politically inconvenient truths or simply to avoid being caught unprepared, it contributes to the general perception that media interviews with politicians are sparring contests.

Communications expert Robert Cialdini calls such pivots "prepared evasions." While he recommends the deft turn "from a bad question to a good answer," he cautions against doing so too abruptly, as this transparently exposes the pivoter's weakness. "Some link, some association must be found to link the two," he says, even if it's a simple acknowledgment of the topic, followed by "I haven't researched that area, but your question brings up another important issue. . . ."[22] What's crucial, Cialdini emphasizes, is that the tactic "not be duplicitous," but rather, forthright and controlled. If you want your audience to trust and respect you, you've got to maintain your authority.

So it is, too, with corporate pivots that shift a company's resources away from failing areas of business toward less visible areas that have more promise. Never show the desperation that's actually motivating the turn. Make the pivot appear seamless, controlled, and intentional.

Examples of successful pivots stud business history. A door-to-door bookseller pivoted to beauty products, and wound up founding Avon Cosmetics. A baking powder company began giving out gum to customers as a premium, but when it became clear that people were buying the baking powder to get the gum, William Wrigley Jr. wisely pivoted into the gum business. And then there's Silicon Valley, where pivots today are practically standard operating procedure.

One of the first there to realize the value of this emergency out was Stewart Butterfield, who, along with his wife, Caterina Fake, and programmer Jason Classon, formed a company in 2002 called Ludicorp. Their product was Game Neverending, a massive multiplayer universe in which users could play indefinitely without winning or losing. Butterfield and his team designed the interface so that players spoke to each other through instant-messaging windows while gaming. They could drag game objects into the IM window and an image of that object would be sent to all members of the chat. It seemed very promising.

In time, Game Neverending did amass a loyal fan base, but Ludicorp was quickly running out of money, and after the dot-com crash, there was little hope of finding venture capital to keep the company alive. "We got to the point," Butterfield recalls, "where the only person who got paid was the one of us who had kids."

Faced with the imminent death of his business, Butterfield studied the dilemma from every angle he could imagine. He realized that, while the game itself was not taking off, the user interface had a whole different kind of potential. It was unique. It worked beautifully. The players loved it. What if he pivoted the company away

$\longrightarrow$ **CONJURE AN OUT** from the now-ending game, to focus on the interface? The bigger question was, how to persuade investors to buy it?

In April 2004, Butterfield was scheduled to speak at the Etech conference in San Diego about some of the technical aspects of Game Neverending. At the last minute, he decided that he and his team would use the forum to unveil the company's new focus. No one knew what they were planning. No one was paying attention. This was their off-beat, a chance to change their trick without anyone's eyes on them.

The Ludicorp team pulled an all-nighter to get the presentation ready. The problem was that the technology Butterfield envisioned was latent in the game, rather than fully developed. The image-sharing program wasn't even close to being ready. A little time reversal was in order. So the team patched together a slide deck to create the illusion that it was all set. The slides showed how users could upload images to the site via email, thereby sharing pictures from their mobile phones. They gave the impression that the team knew exactly what they were doing.

The next day, jaws dropped as Butterfield and Fake described the capabilities of the new company they envisioned, a ground-breaking concept that began as a last-minute leap for survival.

The result of this pivot was named Flickr.

CONCLUSION

On May 16, 1908, at the Ford Opera House in Baltimore, Harry Kellar, the renowned stage illusionist and "Dean of American Magicians," bid farewell to magic. After decades of shows on five continents, Kellar was giving the final performance of his sendoff tour. Sharing the bill was Howard Thurston, twenty years his junior, whom Kellar had anointed as America's next great magician. Posters advertising the event depicted the great illusionist draping the "Mantle of Magic" over his successor's shoulders.

The transfer of the power of illusion is a concept that I embrace, and though I certainly don't wear the mantle, in my own way, with this book, I am passing its benefits on to you.

Whether you employ the power of illusion is up to you, but if you choose to, here are a few tips and reminders to help you make the most of it:

- Wear the mantle well. You now possess information that can put you in front of the competition. It's better to use this information to get a step ahead in your own life than to intentionally cause others to fall behind in theirs. By the same token, your newfound skill set equips you to spot those who would take advantage of you and of others. Stay alert for those who misuse the principles of illusion, and call them out when you find them.

- Start small. As with any field that takes time to master, you'll need to practice. Begin with manageable bites. Professional magicians try their new routines on trusted audiences, often in friends' living rooms. Find your own safe zones and minor challenges to begin experimenting with these principles. Build confidence and familiarity before testing your command of the gap on more significant challenges.

- Highlight your strengths. The beauty of illusion is that the final moments of your audience's experience are under your control. You are the sole author of their takeaways. So think about what is most important for people to remember about you, and make this the end of your story. Work backward from there.

- Engage with your audience. The first magician I ever saw as a boy placed a little red sponge in my hand and made a second one disappear. When I opened my hand two sponges appeared. I was spellbound because the illusionist made me believe that *I* created the miracle. Try to elicit a similar feeling with the people in your life. Experiment with illusions that make your audience feel special, that make them believe the power is in *their* hands.

- Embrace change. Magicians are always evolving. They employ the very latest technologies and leverage current trends to stay a step ahead of the public. Remember, today's status quo is tomorrow's history. So how will you adapt to meet the future? New ideas, new skills, and new directions are the stuff of magic.

CONCLUSION ← ⎯⎯⎯⎯

- Cross-pollinate. As you launch a new business or start a new project, consider the benefits of combining ideas. I did not find my voice in magic until I fused illusion and puzzles. What areas of skill and interest can you cross-pollinate to turbocharge your career?

- Control the reveal. Some magicians believe that the secret behind an illusion is worth exposing if the method is more entertaining than the trick itself. Let's say that you've worked nights and weekends on a presentation that your boss believes has just materialized out of nowhere. If you want recognition for all the hard work, you can disclose the extra hours you put into it, but if you want to appear superhuman, keep that secret close to the vest. Let your objectives guide you.

- Embrace adversity. I'm often asked how magicians cope with YouTube exposing the secrets of magic. The truth is, it doesn't bother us in the least, because the Internet also helps us to widen the gap of illusion. My peers delight in uploading fake tutorials to YouTube or posting false explanations in the comments section. The lesson here for you: Work *within* adversity to turn it into an advantage.

- Be bold. Magicians are confident onstage because everything in their purview is within their control. The same will be true for you as you master the principles of illusion. You'll find that the power of the out and the narrative that you alone command can empower you to take new risks. Reach for that impossible sales goal. Try to land that major client. Remember that no one controls the end of the story but you.

⟶ **CONCLUSION**

As Harry Kellar's final show concluded, the Dean of Magicians walked toward the footlights with his arm around his protégé. Then, with great ceremony and tears in his eyes, Kellar handed his successor his wand.

And now, with one last magical message, I'm passing you my virtual wand. This message comes from the great Houdini. In many ways it is the ultimate principle of illusion:

Your brain is the key that sets you free.

May you use this key well and wisely.

ACKNOWLEDGMENTS

A book on the shelves is an illusion like anything else: the audience does not see all the behind-the-scenes work and support that went into creating the final effect. Thus, I'd like to thank a number of friends and colleagues who believed in this book, regaled me with stories from magic history, assisted me with research, or gave me feedback on paragraphs and pages.

First, I cannot thank enough my agent, Richard Pine, who shepherded this book over the last two years. From the moment I walked into his office (and the subsequent times I've sneaked into it to hide things), I've felt at home. Richard, I am grateful for your trust in this book and my career.

My extraordinary editors at Harper Business, Hollis Heimbouch and Stephanie Hitchcock, transformed this book from a nascent concept to something I am truly proud of. Hollis and Stephanie, you saw the potential in this idea, championed my voice, and guided me every step of the way. I am also fortunate to have such an incredible marketing and publicity team. Thank you to Tina Andreadis, Brian Perrin, Rachel Elinsky, Nikki Baldauf, and Cindy Achar at Harper, and Bebe Lerner at ID-PR. I am sorry that I have ruined magic for all of you.

Thank you to Eliza Rothstein, Alexis Hurley, William Callahan, and everyone at InkWell Management. I promise I'll tell you how I do my tricks after the *next* book.

A couple of professors of prestidigitation kindly offered me their knowledge of magic history: Jon Racherbaumer is wise, encyclopedic, and a true legend. If you are a student of illusion, make a pilgrimage to New Orleans to see him! Bill Goodwin, the librarian at the Magic Castle, knows more about magic than anyone I've ever met. Night after night he pointed me towards gems on the bookshelf. I couldn't have done this without him.

To some of the world's best magicians: Dan White, Blake Vogt, Jonathan Bayme, Francis Menotti, Mike Caveney, Doug McKenzie, John Cox, Kostya Kimlat, Chris Chelko, Justin Willman, Art Benjamin, and Lew Horwitz—thank you all for your time and inspiration. Last, if you were the magician at Bauman Farms in Rochester, New York, in the early '90s, who wowed a wide-eyed half-Chinese kid, please get in touch with me. You started it all.

In particular, I'd like to recognize the brilliant Aimee Liu. This book would not be possible without you, Aimee. Thank you for your mastery of language, your vision, and your sense of humor. Jennifer DeVore, I'm grateful for your insightful and thorough research. I won the lottery by getting to work with you! Hilary Liftin, your insight and macro view of the book were invaluable when this project was just the germ of an idea.

My sophomore year of college, Adam Grant and I formed the Harvard Magic Society. Seven of us entertained at study breaks, arts festivals, and once drove all the way to Connecticut to perform at a bar mitzvah for $200. Adam, I marvel at your accomplishments, and I am grateful for all the advice you've given to me on this book, on business, and in life.

ACKNOWLEDGMENTS ⟵

I'd also like to thank a number of luminaries who graciously gave me their time and feedback: Barry Schwartz, Paul Zak, Jim McGaugh, Scott Johnson, Christopher Carpenter, Simon Sinek, Gary Noesner, Chris Voss, Aryeh Bourkoff, Tony Hsieh, Trevor Traina, Dion Lim, Max Bazerman, Tristan Walker, Edgar Wright, Brad Bird, Molly and Ted Fienning, Adam Bryant, Janet Elkin, Daniel Lubetzky, and the inimitable Will Shortz.

To my dear friends: Aline Brosh McKenna, no one has pushed me harder in my career and life than you have. Thank you for inspiring me, challenging me, and laughing with me. Alex Young, I've relied on your wisdom and calm voice all these years. Thank you for always being there for me. Chris Starr, you've read page after page of this book, and have improved it with every suggestion. But most importantly, you're generous, loyal, genius, and there are three things that should bother you about this sentence.

For their loving encouragement over the years I thank my parents, Tai Kwong and Joanie Rubin, and my brother, Michael. The family members of a magician know all too well the phrase "Hey, can I practice this trick on you?" For decades, you've patiently supported my art. Mom and Dad, thank you for giving me the room to shape this childhood hobby into an exciting career. Michael, when times have been tough, you've always been the first to reassure me that I had a special talent. I am so proud to share this book with all of you.

NOTES

CHAPTER 1

1. James Wood Brown, *An Enquiry into the Life and Legend of Michael Scot* (Edinburgh: David Douglas, 1897), 218–19.

2. Ibid., 164–65.

3. Louisa Compton, Twitter post, June 24, 2016, 6:52 a.m., http://louisa_compton.

4. Adam Bryant, "Always Keep a Few Tricks Up Your Sleeve," *New York Times*, July 24, 2010.

5. Derren Brown, *Tricks of the Mind* (London: Channel 4 Books, 2006), 42.

6. Adam Bryant, "Presto! A Leader," *New York Times*, Corner Office, October 24, 2015.

7. Ingmar Bergman, "Why I Make Movies," *Horizon*, September 1960, reprinted in *DGA Quarterly*, Winter 2012.

8. Dean Robinson, "What's in J. J. Abrams's Mystery Box?," *New York Times*, June 2, 2011.

9. Aimee E. Stahl and Lisa Feigenson, "Observing the Unexpected Enhances Infants' Learning and Exploration," *Science* 348, no. 6230 (April 2, 2015): 91–94.

10. Dawn Perlmutter, "The Politics of Muslim Magic," *Middle East Quarterly*, Spring 2013, 73–80, http://www.meforum.org/3533/islam-magic-witchcraft.

11. Ibid., http://www.meforum.org/3533/islam-magic-witchcraft#_ftn32.

12. Ibid., http://www.meforum.org/3533/islam-magic-witchcraft#_ftn33.

13. Shelby Grad and David Colker, "Nancy Reagan Turned to Astrology in White House to Protect Her Husband," *Los Angeles Times*, March 6, 2016.

14. Michael Curtis, "Magic and Politics," *American Thinker*, January 29, 2016.

15. Michael Beschloss, "David Greenberg's 'Republic of Spin,'" review of *Republic of Spin*, by David Greenberg, *New York Times*, January 20, 2016.

16. "Guest blog: Mr. Houdini Goes to Washington, Part I," Wild About Harry blog, February 8, 2015, http://wildabouthoudini.com.

17. Christopher Maag, "Scam Everlasting: After 25 Years, Debunked Faith Healer Still Preaching Debt Relief Scam," *Business Insider*, September 22, 2011.

18. Scan of Popoff letter: http://www.christianissues.com/trickery.html.

19. Maag, "Scam Everlasting."

20. Maria Konnikova, "Born to Be Conned," *New York Times*, December 5, 2015.

21. "The Man Who Figured Out Madoff's Scheme," *60 Minutes*, March 1, 2009, http://www.cbsnews.com/news/the-man-who-figured-out-mad offs-scheme-27-02-2009/.

22. Mark St. Cyr, "Theranos: Unicorn Valley's Madoff Moment," Mark St. Cyr blog, June 5, 2016, https://markstcyr.com/2016/06/05/thera nos-unicorn-valleys-madoff-moment/.

CHAPTER 2

1. David Price, *Magic: A Pictorial History of Conjurers in the Theater* (New York: Cornwall Books, 1985), 330–31.

2. Rosabeth Moss Kanter, "Instant Success Takes Time," *Harvard Business Review*, November 12, 2008.

3. Dan Charnas, "For a More Ordered Life, Organize Like a Chef," *NPR Morning Edition*, August 11, 2014.

4. Michael Edwards, "The Sphinx and the Spy: The Clandestine World of John Mulholland," *Genii: The Conjurer's Magazine*, April 2001.

5. Rita McGrath and Ian MacMillan, "MarketBusting: Strategies for Exceptional Business Growth," *Harvard Business Review*, March 2005.

6. John Augustine Daly, *Advocacy: Championing Ideas and Influencing Others* (New Haven, CT: Yale University Press, 2011), 178.

7. Karan Girotra and Serguei Netessine, "Four Paths to Business Model Innovation," *Harvard Business Review*, July–August 2014.

8. Robert Greene, *The 48 Laws of Power* (New York: Penguin Books, 1998), 102–3.

9. Ric Merrifield, "The Internet of Things Is Changing How We Manage Customer Relationships," *Harvard Business Review*, June 5, 2015.

10. Ilan Mochari, "The Eisenhower Matrix: How to Choose What to Work on When: Make Use of the Simple—and Presidentially Vetted—Eisenhower Matrix," *Inc.*, March 3, 2014.

11. Ron Friedman, "How to Spend the First 10 Minutes of Your Day," *Harvard Business Review*, June 19, 2014.

12. Charnas, "For a More Ordered Life."

13. Deena Skolnick Weisberg, Kathy Hirsh-Pasek, Roberta Michnick Golinkoff, and Bruce D. McCandliss, "Mise en place: Setting the Stage for Thought and Action," *Trends in Cognitive Science* 18, no. 6 (June 2014): 276–78.

14. Geoffrey L. Cohen, Julio Garcia, Valerie Purdie-Vaughns, Nancy Apfel, and Patricia Brzustoski, "Recursive Processes in Self-Affirmation: Intervening to Close the Minority Achievement Gap," *Science* 324 (April 17, 2009): 400–403.

15. Shawn Setaro, "Dan Charnas: Using Lessons from Great Chefs to Help Us 'Work Clean,'" *Forbes*, April 27, 2016.

CHAPTER 3

1. Significant Objects, http://significantobjects.com/.

2. Fritz Heider and Marianne Simmel, "An Experimental Study of Apparent Behavior," *American Journal of Psychology* 57, no. 2 (April 1944): 243–59.

3. "Aboriginal 'Memories' of Australia's Coastline Go Back More than 7,000 Years," ScienceDaily.com, original source, *Taylor & Francis*, September 17, 2015. https://www.sciencedaily.com/releases/2015/09/1509170 91401.htm.

4. Jennifer Aaker, "Harnessing the Power of Stories: Discussion Guide," Center for the Advancement of Women's Leadership, Stanford University, https://womensleadership.stanford.edu/stories.

5. Jill Suttie, "The Storytelling Animal," review of *The Storytelling Animal: How Stories Make Us Human,* by Jonathan Gottschall, Greater Good Science Center, University of California, Berkeley, June 13, 2012.

6. Paul J. Zak, "How Stories Change the Brain," Greater Good Science Center, University of California, Berkeley, December 17, 2013.

7. Harrison Monarth, "The Irresistible Power of Storytelling as a Strategic Business Tool," *Harvard Business Review,* March 11, 2014.

8. Jill Rosen, "Super Bowl Ads: Stories Beat Sex and Humor, Johns Hopkins Researcher Finds," *Hub,* Johns Hopkins University, January 31, 2014.

9. Steve Cady, "A Brash Captain Keeps the Cup," *New York Times,* September 18, 1977.

10. Malcolm Gladwell, "The Sure Thing: How Entrepreneurs Really Succeed," *New Yorker,* January 18, 2010.

11. Anat Keinan, Jill Avery, and Neeru Paharia, "Capitalizing on the Underdog Effect," *Harvard Business Review,* November 2010.

12. Jean-Eugène Robert-Houdin, *Memoirs of Robert-Houdin, Ambassador, Author and Conjurer* (London: Chapman & Hall, 1859), 177–78.

13. Ibid., 202.

14. Sarah Maslin Nir, "Unwrapping the Mythos of Mast Brothers Chocolate in Brooklyn," *New-York Times,* December 20, 2015.

15. Kate Taylor, "Gourmet Shops' Sales of the Most Hip Chocolate Brand Are Plunging After a Scandal," *Business Insider,* January 19, 2016.

16. Christian Rudder, "The Best Questions for a First Date," *OK Trends,* April 20, 2011, http://blog.okcupid.com/index.php/the-best-questions-for-first-dates/.

17. Eugene Mandel, "How the Napa Earthquake Affected Bay Area Sleepers," Jawbone blog, August 25, 2014, https://jawbone.com/blog/napa-earthquake-effect-on-sleep/.

18. John T. Seaman and George David Smith, "Your Company's History as a Leadership Tool," *Harvard Business Review,* December 2012.

19. Ibid.

NOTES

←

20. "Babiators: Sunglasses That Survive Toddler Terror," *Taking Stock*, Bloomberg TV, May 1, 2014.

21. Molly Fienning, email to the author, July 13, 2016.

22. Ty Montague, "Good Companies Are Storytellers. Great Companies Are Storydoers," *Harvard Business Review*, July 16, 2013.

23. "It Is Only Hypnotism," *Chicago Tribune*, August 9, 1890, http://archives .chicagotribune.com/1890/08/09/page/9/article/it-is-only-hypnotism.

24. Teller, "'The Rise of the Indian Rope Trick': The Grift of the Magi," review of *The Rise of the Indian Rope Trick*, by Peter Lamont, *New York Times Book Review*, February 13, 2005.

25. Donald A. Redelmeier, Joel Katz, and Daniel Kahneman, "Memories of Colonoscopy: A Randomized Trial," *Pain* 104, nos. 1–2 (July 2003): 187–94.

26. Adam Bryant, "Jane Elkin, on Not Letting the Process Defeat the Purpose," *New York Times*, November 8, 2014.

CHAPTER 4

1. Eric R. Waples, "Franklin D. Roosevelt: The Media, His Physical Image, and Teaching Implications" (Master's thesis, College at Brockport, State University of New York, 2013), 43, http://digitalcommons.brock port.edu/cgi/viewcontent.cgi?article=1313&context=ehd_theses.

2. Ibid., 44.

3. "Hiding in Plain Sight," *This American Life*, July 13, 2012, transcript, http://www.thisamericanlife.org/radio-archives/episode/469/transcript.

4. "How Eyes Trick Your Mind," *BBC Future*, January 30, 2015, http:// www.bbc.com/future/bespoke/story/20150130-how-your-eyes-trick-your-mind/.

5. Jeff K. Caird, Kate A. Johnston, Chelsea R. Willness, Mark Asbridge, and Piers Steele, "A Meta-analysis of the Effects of Texting on Driving," *Accident Analysis & Prevention* 71 (October 2014): 311–18.

6. David L. Strayer, Frank A. Drews, and Dennis J. Crouch, "Fatal Distraction? A Comparison of the Cell-Phone Driver and the Drunk Driver," Applied Cognition Lab, University of Utah, 2003.

7. Peter Mundy and Lisa Newell, "Attention, Joint Attention, and Social Cognition," National Center for Biotechnology Information, *Current Directions in Psychological Science* 16, no. 5 (October 1, 2007): 269–74.

8. Bryant, "Presto!"

9. "Moral Decisions Can Be Influenced by Eye Tracking," ScienceDaily
.com, original source Lund University, March 18, 2015, http://www.sci
encedaily.com/releases/2015/03/150318101434.htm.

10. "Two Sides of the Same Coin: Speech and Gesture Mutually Interact
to Enhance Comprehension," ScienceDaily.com, original source Association for Psychological Science, January 6, 2010, http://www.science
daily.com/releases/2010/01/100105143730.htm.

11. Graham Davies and Sarah Hine, "Change Blindness and Eyewitness
Testimony," *Journal of Psychology: Interdisciplinary and Applied* 141, no.
4 (2007): 423–34.

12. Daniel Simons, "But Did You See the Gorilla? The Problem with Inattentional Blindness," *Smithsonian Magazine*, September 2012.

13. Angela Wilkinson and Roland Kupers, "Living in the Futures," *Harvard
Business Review*, May 2013.

14. Roger Dooley, "The Power of New," Neuromarketing blog, July 26,
2008, http://www.neurosciencemarketing.com/blog/articles/the-pow
er-of-new.htm.

15. B. P. Davis and E. S. Knowles, "A Disrupt-Then-Reframe Technique of
Social Influence," *Journal of Personality and Social Psychology* 76, no. 2
(1999): 192–99.

16. James Allen, "Living Differentiation," *Harvard Business Review*, March
21, 2012.

17. Ethan Bernstein, "Why We Hide Some of Our Best Work," *Harvard
Business Review*, September 24, 2014.

18. "Use Small Plates to Lose Weight," ScienceDaily.com, original source
Cornell Food and Brand Lab, January 12, 2016, https://www.science
daily.com/releases/2016/01/160112091636.htm.

19. Jacob Goldstein, "The Secret to Club Stores' Success: Breaking the Rules
of Retail," *NPR All Things Considered*, September 30, 2015, transcript,
http://www.npr.org/2015/09/30/444790866/the-secret-to-club-stores-
success-breaking-the-rules-of-retail.

20. April Joyner, "Case Study: Keep Your Day Job and Start a Business,"
Inc., November 1, 2012, http://www.inc.com/april-joyner/bootstrap-
keep-your-day-job-start-a-business.html.

NOTES

←

21. Natalie Clarkson, "Why Did Richard Branson Start an Airline?," Virgin.com, October 1, 2014, https://www.virgin.com/travel/why-did-richard-branson-start-an-airline.

22. Anna Mikulak, "All About Awe: Science Explores How Life's Small Marvels Elevate Cognition and Emotion," *Observer* 28, no. 4 (April 2015).

23. D. Keltner and J. Haidt, "Approaching Awe, a Moral, Spiritual, and Aesthetic Emotion," *Cognition & Emotion* 17 (2003): 297–314, cited in Melanie Rudd, Kathleen D. Vohs, and Jennifer Aaker, "Awe Expands People's Perception of Time, Alters Decision Making, and Enhances Well-Being," *Psychological Science* 23, no. 10 (2012): 1130–36.

CHAPTER 5

1. "But You Are Free (BYAF)," ChangingMinds.Org, http://changingminds.org/techniques/general/sequential/but_you_are_free.htm.

2. John Beshears and Francesca Gino, "Leaders as Decision Architects," *Harvard Business Review*, May 2015.

3. Theresa Johnston and Balaji Prabhakar, "Doesn't Anybody Care About This Traffic?!," *Insights by Stanford Business*, April 16, 2014.

4. Phil Rockrohr, "Thaler Explains How 'Choice Architecture' Makes the World a Better Place," *ChicagoBooth News*, May 16, 2008, http://www.chicagobooth.edu/news/2008ManCon/01-thaler.aspx.

5. David Halpern et al., "EAST: Four Simple Ways to Apply Behavioural Insights," Behavioural Insights Team, http://www.behaviouralinsights.co.uk/wp-content/uploads/2015/07/BIT-Publication-EAST_FA_WEB.pdf.

6. Brigid Schulte, "No Vacation Nation? One Company Gives Workers $7,500 to Unplug and Get Away," *Washington Post*, October 23, 2014.

7. Beshears and Gino, "Leaders as Decision Architects."

8. Halpern et al., "EAST."

9. Maanvi Singh, "Apps Can Speed the Search for Love, but Nothing Beats a Real Date," NPR, February 12, 2015.

10. Beshears and Gino, "Leaders as Decision Architects."

11. Rockrohr, "Thaler Explains How 'Choice Architecture' Makes the World a Better Place."

12. James Tozer, "Why Shoppers Find It So Hard to Escape from Ikea:

Flatpack Furniture Stores Are 'Designed Just Like a Maze,'" *Daily Mail*, January 24, 2011.

13.   "Apple Is Ditching the Standard Headphone Jack to Screw Consumers and the Planet," SumOfUs.org, https://action.sumofus.org/a/iphone-headphone-jack/.

14.   Michael Paoletta, "Reznor Adopts Unusual Web Campaign for New Album," Reuters, April 2, 2007, http://www.reuters.com/article/us-nineinchnails-idUSN0233620220070402.

15.   "Audiences Are Primed for Discovery," 42 Entertainment, http://42entertainment.com/.

CHAPTER 6

1.   "Prime Minister Winston Churchill Debate in the House of Commons," *Parliamentary Debates, House of Commons Official Report*, November 11, 1942.

2.   "The 3132 Signal Company: The Sonic Deceivers," The Ghost Army: World War II's Artists of Deception, http://www.ghostarmy.org/index.php?page=bio&category=03--Inside_the_23rd&display=415.

3.   Hermann Bulf, Scott P. Johnson, and Eloisa Valenza, "Visual Statistical Learning in the Newborn Infant," *Cognition* 121 (2011): 127–32.

4.   Hillary Mayell, "Babies Recognize Faces Better Than Adults, Study Says," *National Geographic News*, May 22, 2005.

5.   Alex Bellos, "And Now for Something Completely Random," DailyMail.co.uk, December 7, 2010, http://www.dailymail.co.uk/home/moslive/article-1334712/Humans-concept-randomness-hard-understand.html.

6.   Michael Shermer, "Patternicity: Finding Meaningful Patterns in Meaningless Noise," *Scientific American*, December 1, 2008.

7.   Gene Weingarten, "Pearls Before Breakfast: Can One of the Nation's Great Musicians Cut Through the Fog of a D.C. Rush Hour? Let's Find Out," *Washington Post*, April 8, 2007.

8.   "Ex Machina Tinder Turing Test," ShortyAwards.com, http://shortyawards.com/8th/ex-machina.

9.   Charles Duhigg, *The Power of Habit: Why We Do What We Do in Life and Business* (New York: Random House, 2012), 34.

10.   Ibid., 57.

NOTES   ←————

11. Nicola Twilley, "Accounting for Taste: How Packaging Can Make Food More Flavorful," *New Yorker*, November 2, 2015.

12. Blake Evans-Pritchard, "Aiming to Reduce Cleaning Costs," *Works That Work* no.1 (Winter 2013), https://worksthatwork.com/1/urinal-fly.

13. Amy Webb, "TED Talk: How I Hacked Online Dating," TED.com, filmed April 2013, http://www.ted.com/talks/amy_webb_how_i_hacked_online_dating.

14. Richard H. Thaler and Cass R. Sunstein, *Nudge: Improving Decisions About Health, Wealth, and Happiness* (New Haven, CT: Yale University Press, 2008), 37.

15. Farhad Manjoo, "Facebook, a News Giant That Would Rather Show Us Baby Pictures," *New York Times*, June 29, 2016.

16. Adam Mosseri, "Building a Better News Feed for You," Facebook Newsroom, June 29, 2016, http://newsroom.fb.com/news/2016/06/building-a-better-news-feed-for-you/.

17. Jonathan Berger, "How Music Hijacks Our Perception of Time," Nautilus.com, January 23, 2014, http://nautil.us/issue/9/time/how-music-hijacks-our-perception-of-time.

18. David Lumb, "Indulge in Your Feels at Glade's Museum of Feelings," November 25, 2015, http://www.fastcocreate.com/3053990/indulge-in-your-feels-at-glades-museum-of-feelings.

19. Ruth Davenport, "Drake Song Hotline Bling Spoofed by RCMP as Reminder of Emergency Vehicle Law," CBCnews.com, April 20, 2016, http://www.cbc.ca/news/canada/nova-scotia/rcmp-music-video-drake-hotline-bling-1.3545494.

20. Hamdi Ulukaya, "Chobani's Founder on Growing a Start-Up Without Outside Investors," *Harvard Business Review*, October 2013.

21. Wikiquote.org, https://en.wikiquote.org/wiki/Arthur_Koestler.

22. Scott Weems, *Ha! The Science of When We Laugh and Why* (New York: Basic Books, 2014), 158.

23. Cora Daniels, "Mr. Coffee: The Man Behind the $4.75 Frappuccino Makes the 500," *Fortune*, April 14, 2003.

24. "Tesco Builds Virtual Shops for Korean Commuters," Telegraph.co.uk, June 27, 2011, http://www.telegraph.co.uk/technology/mobile-phones/8601147/Tesco-builds-virtual-shops-for-Korean-commuters.html.

25.   Stephanie Mlot, "Peapod's Virtual Grocery Store Hits the Road," PCMag
      .com, July 4, 2013, http://www.pcmag.com/article2/0,2817,2421343,00
      .asp.

26.   Shan Li, "How Retail Stores Are Using Virtual Reality to Make Shop-
      ping More Fun," *Los Angeles Times*, April 10, 2016.

CHAPTER 7

1.   Daniel G. Waldron, George Johnstone, and Nick Ruggiero, *Blackstone,
      a Magician's Life: The World and Magic Show of Harry Blackstone, 1885–
      1965* (Glenwood, IL: D. Meyer Magic Books, 1999), 141–43.

2.   Milbourne Christopher, *The Illustrated History of Magic* (New York:
      Crowell, 1973), 374.

3.   Stephen L. Macknik and Susana Martinez-Conde, *Sleights of Mind:
      What the Neuroscience of Magic Reveals About Our Everyday Deceptions*
      (New York: Henry Holt, 2010), 137–38.

4.   Charles Hopkins, *"Outs," Precautions and Challenges for Ambitious Card
      Workers* ([N.p.]: Charles H. Hopkins, 1940), 10–11.

5.   Elie Dolgin, "Publication Bias Continues Despite Clinical-Trial Reg-
      istration," Nature.com, September 11, 2009, http://www.nature.com/
      news/2009/090911/full/news.2009.902.html.

6.   Frederick F. Reichheld, "Learning from Customer Defections," *Harvard
      Business Review*, March–April 1996.

7.   "Organizations Learn More from Failure than Success, Study Finds;
      Knowledge Gained from Failure Lasts Longer," ScienceDaily.com, orig-
      inal source University of Colorado Denver, August 24, 2010, https://
      www.sciencedaily.com/releases/2010/08/100823162322.htm.

8.   J. K. Rowling, "The Fringe Benefits of Failure, and the Importance
      of Imagination," Harvard Commencement Speech, HarvardGazette
      .com transcript, June 5, 2008, http://news.harvard.edu/gazette/
      story/2008/06/text-of-j-k-rowling-speech/.

9.   "Richard Russo & Jenny Boylan on Plot Twists in Books—and Life,"
      Studio 360, May 19, 2016, http://www.wnyc.org/story/richard-rus
      so-jenny-boylan-everybodys-fool/.

10.   David Collis, "Lean Strategy," *Harvard Business Review*, March 2016.

11.   "Remembering Robert R. Taylor, Founder of Minnetonka Corp., Dead

at 77," BusinessWire.com, September 10, 2013, http://www.business wire.com/news/home/20130910006284/en/Remembering-Robert-R.-Taylor-Founder-Minnetonka-Corp.

12. Robert B. Cialdini, "Professionally Responsible Communication with the Public: Giving Psychology a Way," *Personality and Social Psychology Bulletin* 23, no. 7 (July 1997): 675–83.

13. Michel Villette and Catherine Vuillermot, *From Predators to Icons: Exposing the Myth of the Business Hero* (DigitalCommons@ILR Press, 2009), 6.

14. Gladwell, "The Sure Thing."

15. Ben Zimmer, "Iterate," *New York Times Magazine*, June 11, 2010.

16. James Surowiecki, "The Open Secret of Success: Toyota Production System," *New Yorker*, May 12, 2008.

17. Rita McGrath, "Failing by Design," *Harvard Business Review*, April 2011.

18. Andrew Winston, "Resilience in a Hotter World," *Harvard Business Review,* April 2014.

19. Jim Steinmeyer, *The Glorious Deception: The Double Life of William Robinson* (New York: Carroll & Graf, 2005), 220.

20. Christopher Stahl, "Outdoing Ching Ling Foo," in *Performing Magic on the Western Stage: From the Eighteenth Century to the Present*, edited by Francesca Coppa, Lawrence Haas, and James Peck (New York: Palgrave Macmillan), 152.

21. Fred Keating as told to George Bailey, "What Magicians Do When Magical Tricks Go Wrong," *Modern Mechanics and Inventions*, May 1932, reprinted by ModernMechanix.com, February 4, 2009, http://blog.modernmechanix.com/what-magicians-do-when-magical-tricks-go-wrong/.

22. Robert B. Cialdini, "Professionally Responsible Communication with the Public: Giving Psychology a Way," *Personality and Social Psychology Bulletin* 23, no. 7 (July 1997): 675–83.

←

ABOUT THE AUTHOR

DAVID KWONG is a magician and *New York Times* crossword puzzle constructor. He holds a degree in history from Harvard, where he studied the history of magicians. Kwong was the head magic consultant on the worldwide hit *Now You See Me* and is the secret code adviser on NBC's *Blindspot*. Other films he has consulted on include *Mission: Impossible—Rogue Nation*, *The Imitation Game*, and *The Magnificent Seven*. A TED Talk favorite, Kwong regularly lectures and performs for companies worldwide. He lives in Los Angeles.